IMAGE COMICS PRESENTS

FLIGHT

VOLUME TWO

TO KAREN..

..♡KEAN
2007

CONTENTS

Editor/Art Director - Kazu Kibuishi
Asst. Editors - Kean Soo and Phil Craven
Cover - Chris Appelhans
Back Cover - Jake Parker
Contents Page Painting - Catia Chien
Associate - Alfred Moscola

inner
sanctum
Michel Gagné

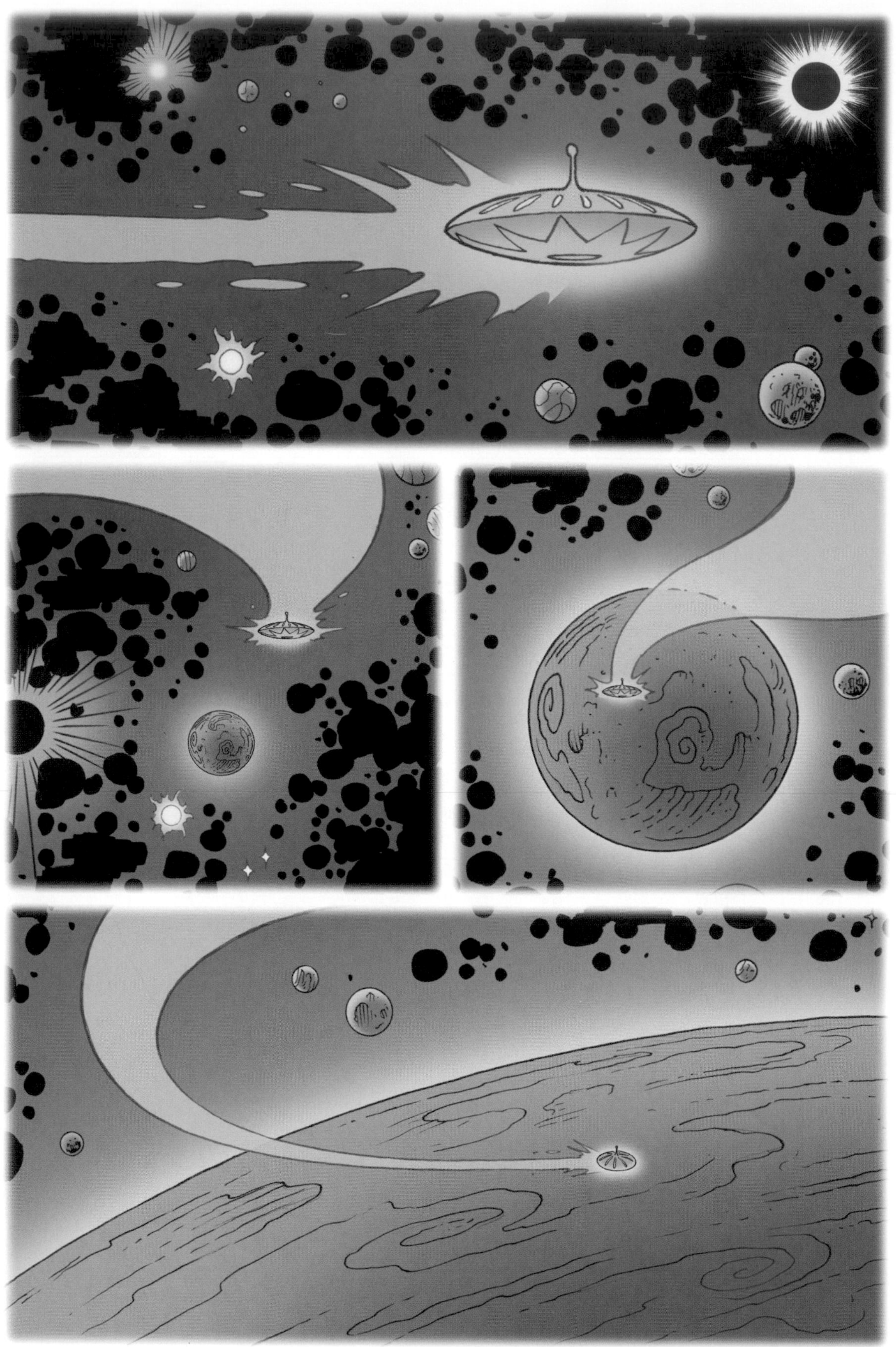

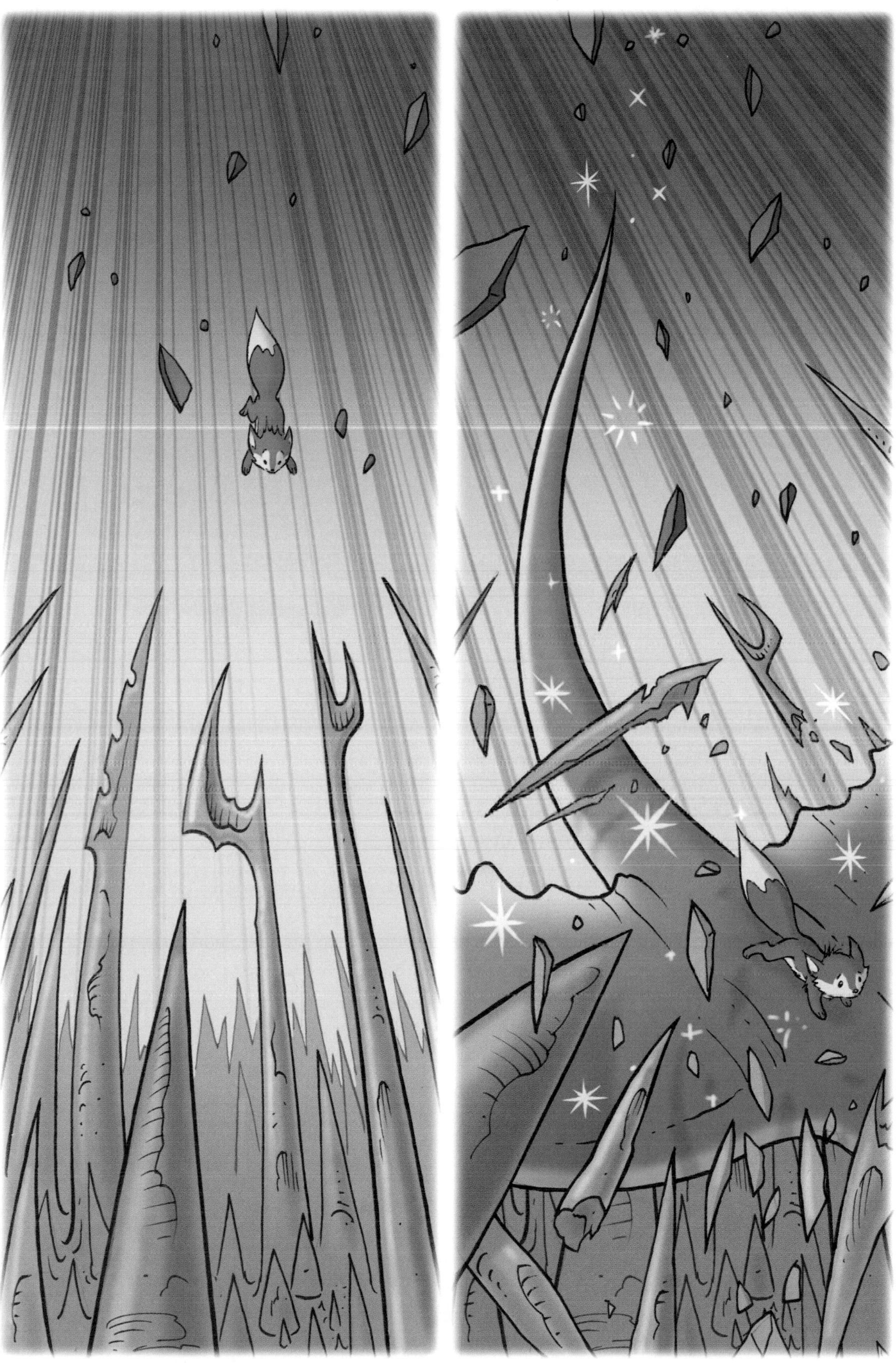

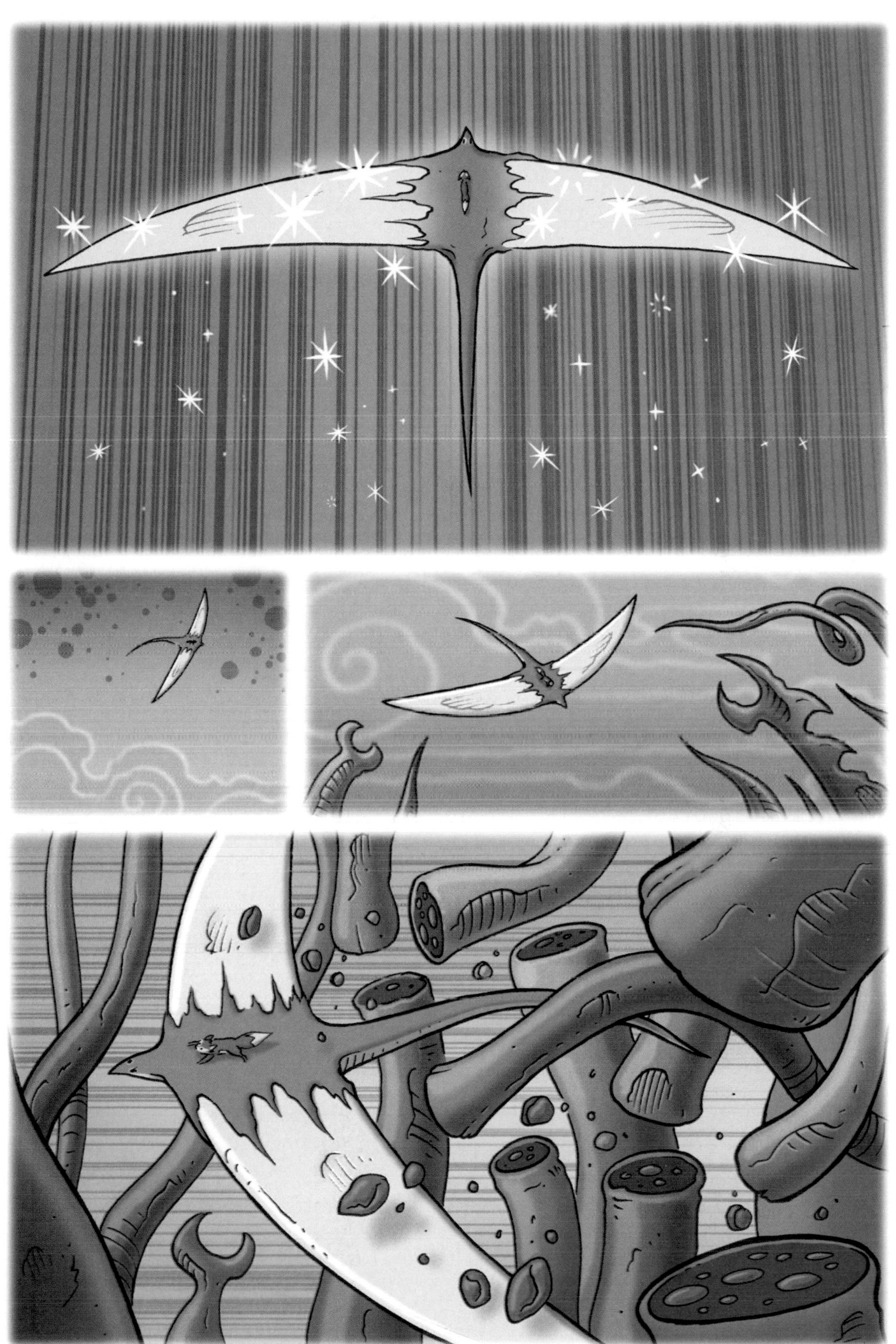

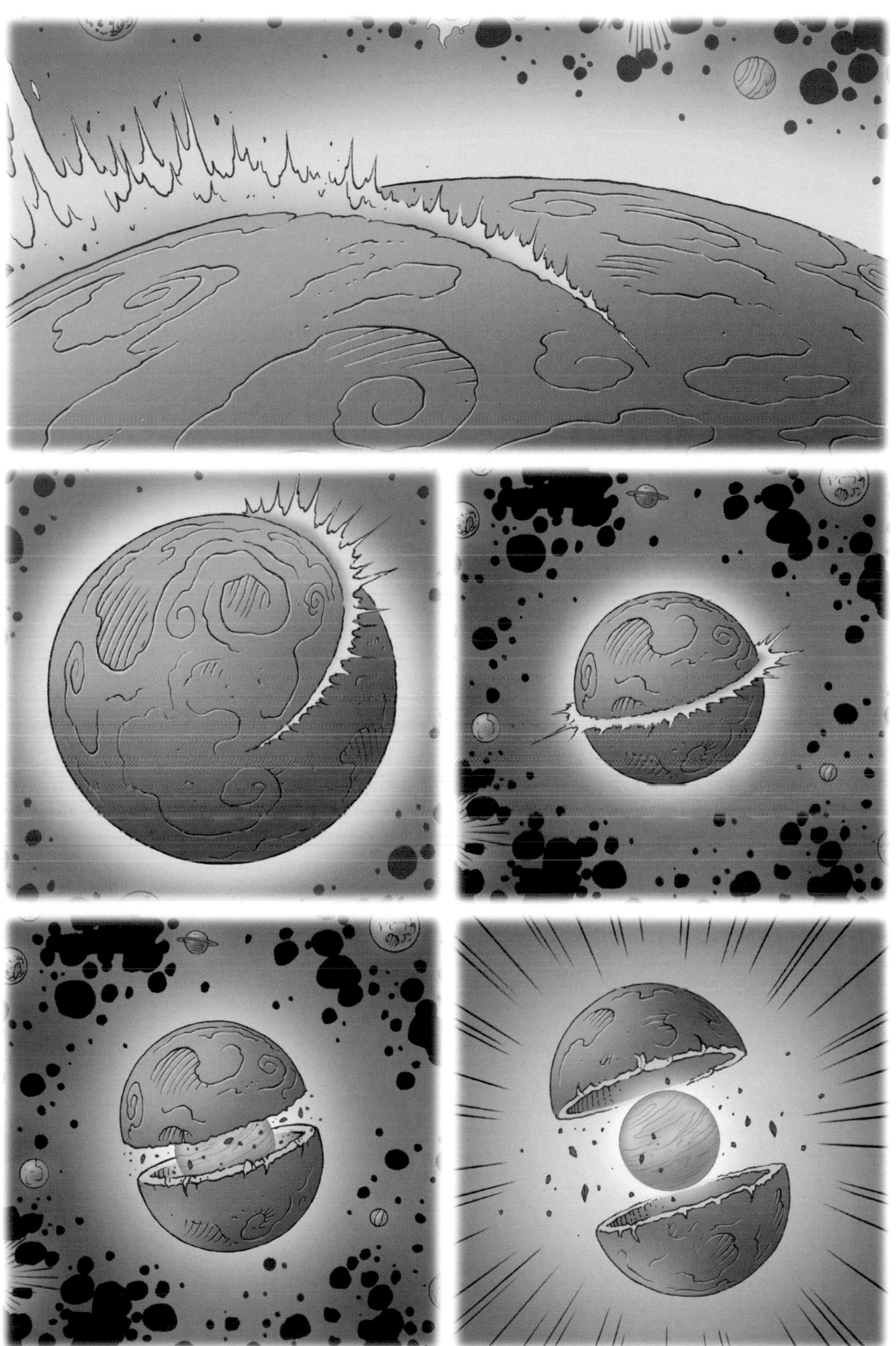

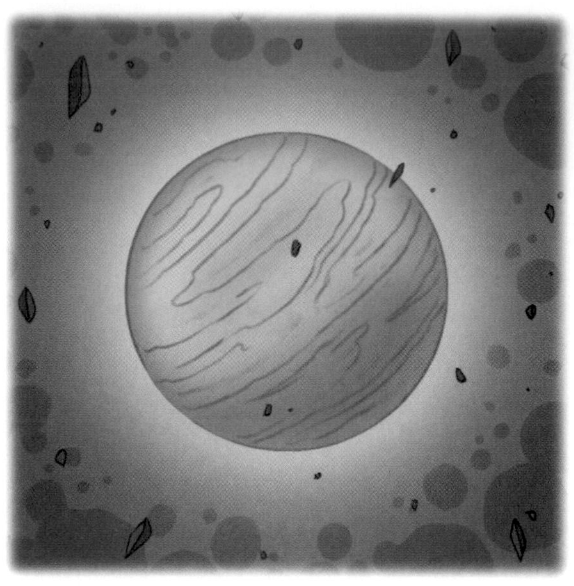

Solomon Fix

by

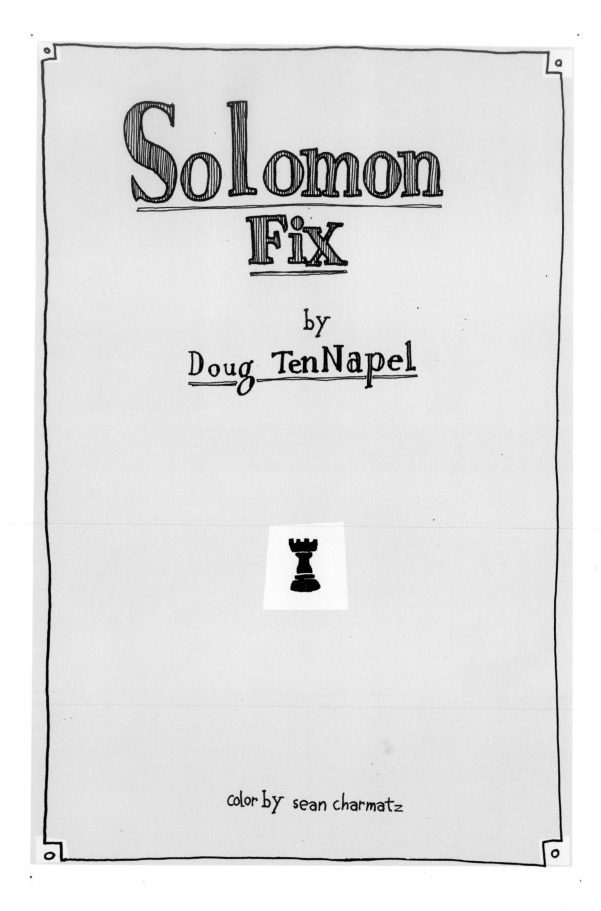

Doug TenNapel

color by sean charmatz

LET US SEE... AM I FORGETTING ANYTHING FOR MY TEA-PARTY TODAY?

I NEED TO BUY: CRUMPETS, BUTTER, PECANS, BLACK OLIVES, BOILED EGGS, CHIP-BUTTY AND OTHER ENGLISH TREATS.

I SHOULD KEEP THE CONSUMABLES ON THE LIGHT SIDE OR MY GUESTS WILL THINK I AM OAFISH.

WELL, MY COUSIN DONKEY IS ARRIVING TODAY, SO I'M GOING TO CELEBRATE BY THROWING AN EXQUISITE TEA PARTY THIS AFTERNOON AT MY HUMBLE ESTATE.
WOULD YOU AND YOUR HAT LIKE TO JOIN US?
NAH.
OKEY -DOKE. GOOD-BYE, ELLIS.

AH, I RECALL THE HAPLESS DAYS OF YOUTH WHEN COUSIN MIKE AND I FRITTERED THE DAY AWAY ON A HEARTY GAME OF CHESS OR DUNGEONS AND DRAGONS.

AND NOW POOR COUSIN MIKE GOT A KICK IN THE CRANIUM BY A ROGUE DONKEY.

MIKE LOST ALL RECOLLECTION OF BEING A FELINE AND NOW HE INSISTS ON BEING CALLED "DONKEY."

HELLO FREQUENT CUSTOMER SOLOMON!
SOL, MAY I SHOW YOU A FEW OF OUR MOST GENEROUS DISCOUNTS WE HAVE TODAY?
OKAY, SHOPKEEPER PHIL. I HAVE A LIST OF GOODS I NEED WHICH I HOPE WILL CORRESPOND WITH YOUR GENEROUS DISCOUNTS.
RIGHT THIS WAY NOW. IMPORTED FROM THE DEPTHS OF THE AFRICAN JUNGLE...

... COMES THIS AMAAAAAZING PRODUCT...
SHOPKEEPER PHIL, THE SIGN SAYS THAT THIS IS APE DUNG.
APE DUNG FROM AFRICA

THAT'S CORRECT! IT IS A GLORIOUS AND HEARTY SUPPLY OF GENUINE APE DUNG!
BUT I DO NOT NEED ANY APE DUNG.

OH SOLOMON! LIFE IS TOO GLORIOUS TO REDUCE ITS PLEASURES TO MERE NEEDS. WHAT ABOUT YOUR WANTS? ARE YOU GOING TO IGNORE YOUR WANTS?
BUT I DO NOT WANT ANY APE DUNG EITHER.

YOU DON'T WANT ANY APE DUNG.

OKAY, TWO FOR ONE! I'LL CUT YOU A GREAT DEAL BECAUSE YOU'RE SUCH A LOYAL PATRON.
I WOULD NOT WANT APE DUNG IF IT WERE FREE!

FINE, SOL. WE'LL JUST WAIT FOR YOUR TASTES TO REFINE BEFORE WE MENTION APE DUNG AGAIN.
NO OFFENSE, SHOPKEEPER PHIL. I'M SURE IT IS THE FINEST APE DUNG AVAILABLE TO MORTALS. BUT I AM SHOPPING FOR A TEA PARTY AND MY PLANS FOR THIS TEA PARTY ARE DEVOID OF APE DUNG.

NEW PRODUCT
MELON

I AM LOOKING FOR BUTTER.

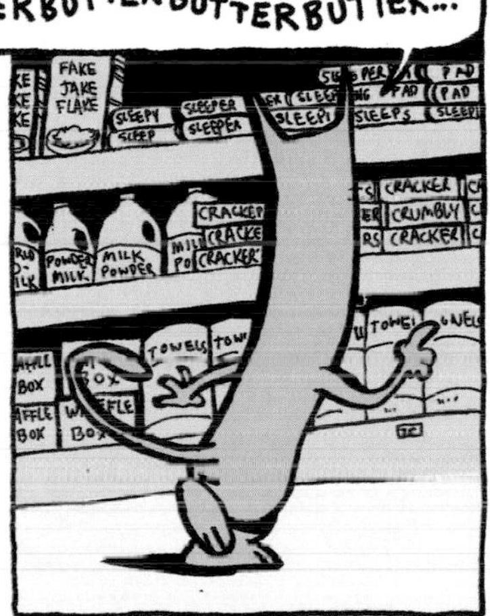
BUTTERBUTTERBUTTERBUTTERBUTTER...

BUTTER!

SO MANY LOVELY BRANDS TO CHOOSE. I WILL CONSIDER PRICE AS I DECIDE.
LET US SEE.
JO-JO BRAND BUTTER IS TWO DOLLARS, THE EQUAL PORTION OF BUTTERFLY BRAND BUTTER COSTS EIGHT DOLLARS.

!

BUT BUTTERFLY BRAND BUTTER FEATURES AN ELEGANT ILLUSTRATION OF A RED ADMIRAL BUTTERFLY RIGHT ON THE LID!
BUTTERFLY BRAND BUTTER

PERHAPS I POSSESS A DISCOUNT COUPON FOR BUTTERFLY BRAND BUTTER!
FLIP
FLIP
FLIP
FLIP

COUPONS

50¢
50¢
50¢ OFF BUTTERFLY BRAND BUTTER
(1 POUND OR LARGER)
IMIT ONE PER COUPON PER CUSTOMER.
Y NOT BE COMBINED WITH ANY OTHER COUPON,
COUNT OR PROMOTION. SALES TAX NOT INCLUDED. GOOD
RTICIPATING LOCATIONS ONLY. VOID
TED. OFFER VALID THROUGH

HAPPY COUPON DANCE! HAPPY COUPON DANCE!

DOUBLE-CHECK EXPIRATION DATE! DOUBLE-CHECK EXPIRATION DATE! IT IS STILL A VALID COUPON!

SECOND HALF OF THE HAPPY COUPON DANCE! SECOND HALF OF THE HAPPY COUPON DANCE!

NOW TO RETRIEVE THE REST OF THE DELICACIES ON MY GROCERY LIST!
MA'AM, CAN I INTEREST YOU IN SOME APE DUNG?
ON SALE
TODAY ONLY!

LA LA LA
LAAAAA
LA LA!

LA LA!

LA!

...I LOVE TO WATCH PIPE SMOKE
DRIFT AWAY...

...LIKE SO MANY SECONDS
IN A DAY...

SNIFF!!

SNIFF
SNIFFFF!

...A BUTTERFLY LIKES TO
FLUTTER BY...

...NE'ER A THOUGHT TOWARD PASSERS BY.

WHAM!!

DARN! MY ARM IS ASLEEP.
WEIRD TINGLE! WEIRD TINGLE!
MY APPENDAGES ARE NEAR EXPIRATION!

I AM NOW READY TO GET READY!

ONE TABLE SPOON OF BUTTER.

REAL CHEFS USE APPROXIMATE MEASUREMENTS SO THE FOOD PREPARATORY PROCESS REMAINS ORGANIC.

FLIP

SUCH A TENACIOUS APPROXIMATE TABLE SPOON OF BUTTERFLY BRAND BUTTER!

FLIP
FLIP
FLIP
FLIP

FLIP!
WOOPS.

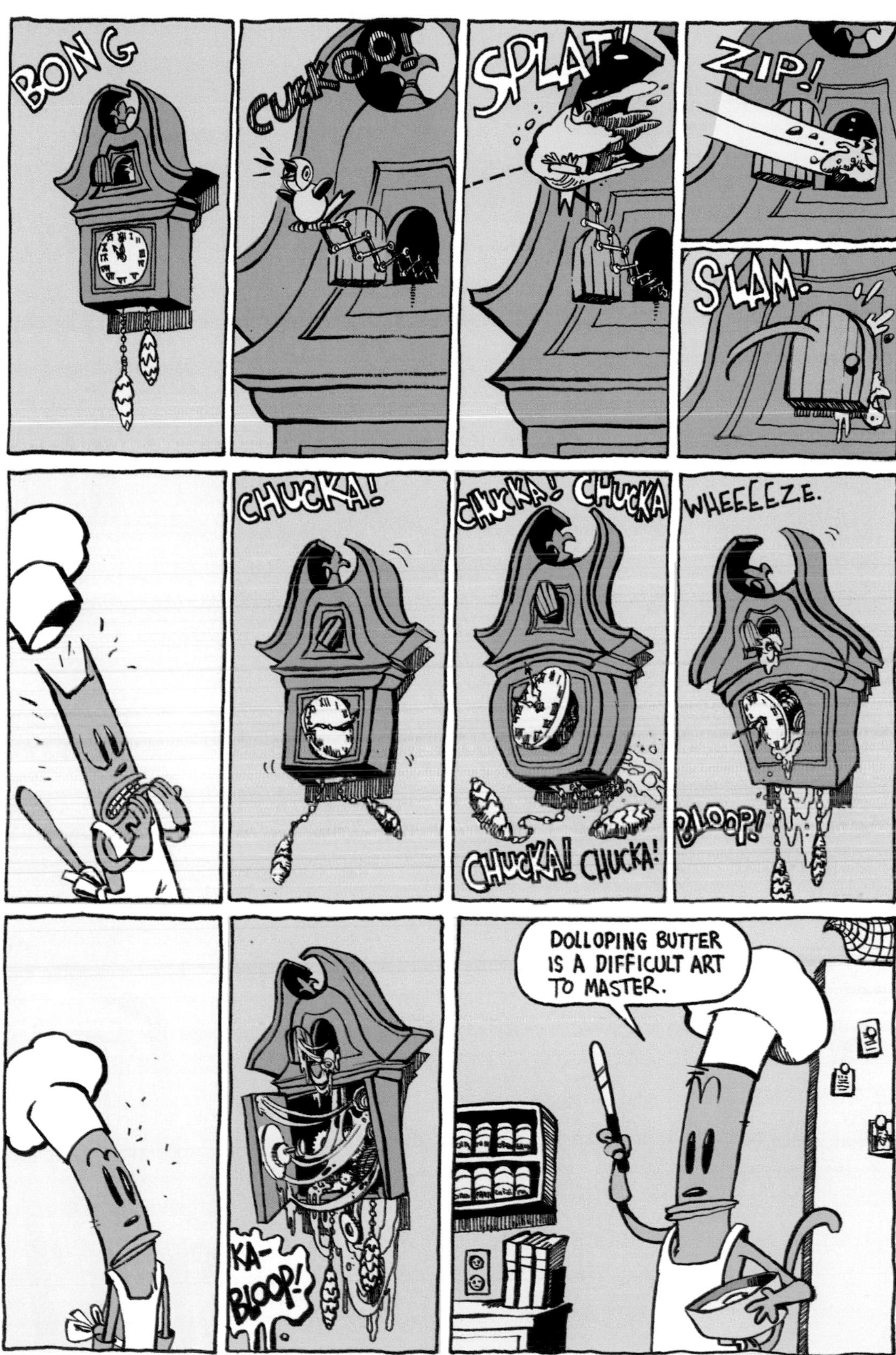
BONG
CUCKOO!
SPLAT!
ZIP!
SLAM.
CHUCKA!
CHUCKA! CHUCKA
CHUCKA! CHUCKA!
WHEEEEZE.
BLOOP!
KA-BLOOP!
DOLLOPING BUTTER IS A DIFFICULT ART TO MASTER.

MUCH LATER:

THESE OYSTERS ROCKEFELLER WILL BE THE PERFECT COMPLIMENT TO MY SWISS-CARAWAY TWISTS.

JEFF AND FLOOBIE WELCOME! PLEASE WIPE YOUR FEET.
HI SOL.
SOL, SOL, CHINA-DOLL!

ENJOY THIS ARRAY OF CHOICE HORS D'OEUVRES.
SO FANCY.
ALL I SEE IS THE EDGE OF THE TABLE! BUT IT LOOKS FANCY AS FAR AS TABLE EDGES GO.
BLUE CHEESE BALL
CHICKEN LIVER PÂTÉ
PEANUTS
RUMAKI

DING DONG
MORE COMPANY!

COMING!!

STINKS THE FLY AND HERKANUDER! ENTER! ENTER! PLEASE WIPE YOUR FEET.
WHO LET THE FLY IN?!
GREETINGS, SOLOMON.

STINKS, I PREPARED A SPECIAL PLATE OF EGG SHELLS AND MELON RINDS ON THE LITTLE ARMOIRE.

DING DONG!

HELLO OREK, SCABBY-BEAR AND CHUMPIE! PLEASE, WIPE YOUR FEET.
WHERE'S THE FOOD.

ALL OF MY ACQUAINTANCES APPEAR TO BE CONTENT WITH THE FESTIVITIES AND THE CONSUMABLES SEEM PRESENT IN VIRTUAL UBIQUITY.

DING-DONG!
THAT MUST BE COUSIN DONKEY!

THE WHOLE WORLD HAS TURNED INTO A COLOSSAL MOUNT OF HAIR AND FANG!
GRRRR.

GRAAAAR!!
URSUS HORRIBILIS! SHOO! SHOO BEAR! SHOO!

WILL YOU AT LEAST WIPE YOUR FEET?!
BLAH!
EAT SOL FIRST! HE IS THE CLOSEST THING TO CHICKEN!

MR. BEAR, PLEASE DO NOT CONSUME ME!

HERE, TRY A SPINACH PHYLLO TRIANGLE!

I MAKE THEM WITH BUTTERFLY BRAND BUTTER.
CHEW CHOMP CHOMP

YOU SHOULD TRY SOME OF THAT MARINATED CHEESE AND OLIVES.

BE CAREFUL OF THOSE TOOTHPICKS!
GULP!

REST YOUR HULKING BONES IN THIS LUXURIOUS CHAIR!

TEA?

THHH... THHH...

...THHHAYNK...

..YEEEEO OOOOO.

YOU ARE WELCOME.

DING-DONG!
COUSIN DONKEY!

WHO WILL CONTINUE TO FEED OUR CARNIVOROUS GUEST?
I WILL!
ME TOO!

MR. BEAR, I NEED TO ANSWER THE DOOR... DO NOT EAT THE GUESTS!
SIP.

HOLD ON FOR ONE MOMENT MY COUSIN DONKEY!

DONKEY?

ME DONKEY.
DO YOU REMEMBER ME? DONKEY, I AM YOUR OLD COUSIN SOLOMON FIX!

SOLOMON.

DONKEY, COME INSIDE AND MASTICATE SOME FOOD!
I HAVE A FEW PEERS YOU SHOULD MEET.

I'M GOING TO WALK THE MILKY WHITE WAY—

GRAARRAARR RAAAH!
...ONE OF THESE DAYS!!
MAY I PLEASE HAVE YOUR ATTENTION?!
THIS IS MY COUSIN DONKEY!
HEE HAW!!
SOMETHING'S WRONG WITH THAT BOY.

HEE-HAW!!

HEE HAW!

IT'S LATE. WE'D BETTER GO!

GRAA-
BYE, SOL.
I'LL SEE YOU LATER, SOLOMON.

NICE PARTY. ABOUT YOUR COUSIN DONKEY...

...RUN FOR YOUR LIFE! HE'S A HIDEOUS MONSTER!

SLAM!

WE HAVE BEEN STANDING HERE FOR TWO HOURS WITH NO INTERRACTION. WHEN WE WERE YOUNGER, WE ALWAYS FOUND FUN THINGS TO DO.

BEHOLD! THE VERY CHESS SET WE FREQUENTED IN OUR YOUTH.

DONKEY! YOU HAVE BEGUN WITHOUT PROMPTING!
PLOP!

YOU BROUGHT OUT YOUR KING'S PAWN! THAT IS A GOOD MOVE, DONKEY!

I WILL BRING OUT MY KING'S PAWN.

YOU BROUGHT OUT YOUR KNIGHT. HMMM...
PLOP!

YOU MOVED YOUR SECOND KNIGHT, JUST LIKE-
...JUST LIKE...

DONKEY! I JUST REALIZED SOMETHING!

YOU ARE PLAYING JUST THE WAY YOU DID BEFORE YOU HAD YOUR ACCIDENT!

PERHAPS THIS IS A VALID TECHNIQUE TO TRANSFORM "COUSIN DONKEY" BACK INTO "COUSIN MIKE"!

YOU WILL LIKELY BRING YOUR BISHIP INTO ACTION NEXT.
SUCH A CUNNING MANEUVER MUST BE PARRIED BY A STALWART DEFENSE!
THE END
D. TENNAPEL

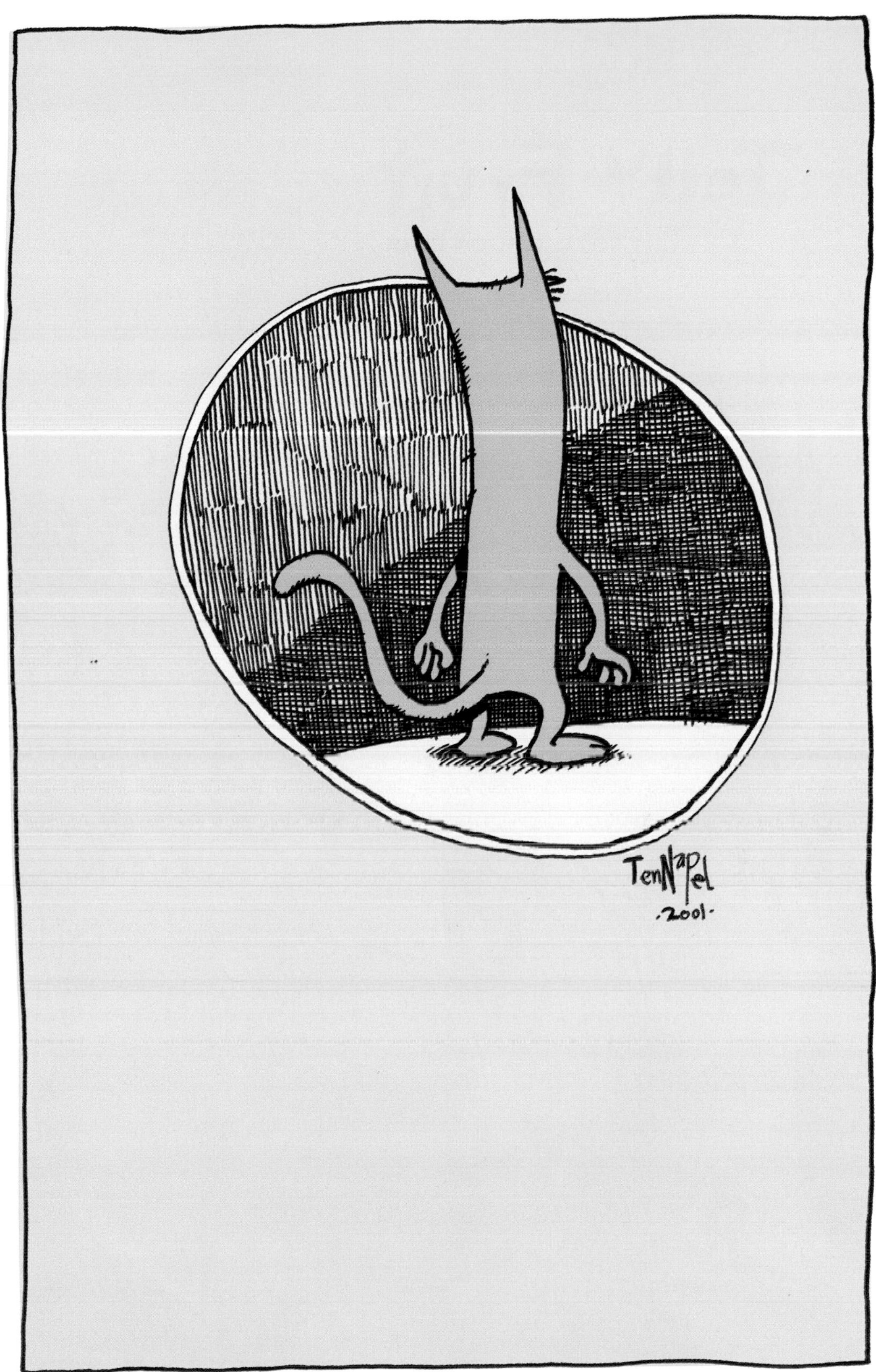
TenNapel
·2001·

JellY Fruit
by: Catia Chien

on the way home one day
I ran into a GIANT who
eats little children
Luckily I was
quick on my feet
ROOOAR

I ran as fast as I could until I found a good hiding place
SIGH

PURRRRR!
!?
PURRRR
PURR
SHHHH
SHHH!!!
YOU DON'T WANT THE GIANT TO FIND US DO YOU?
Meow
ROOOOAR!

SNIFF
SNIFF
SNIFF SNIFF
SNIFF
SQUISH
SQUISH

The end 

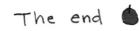

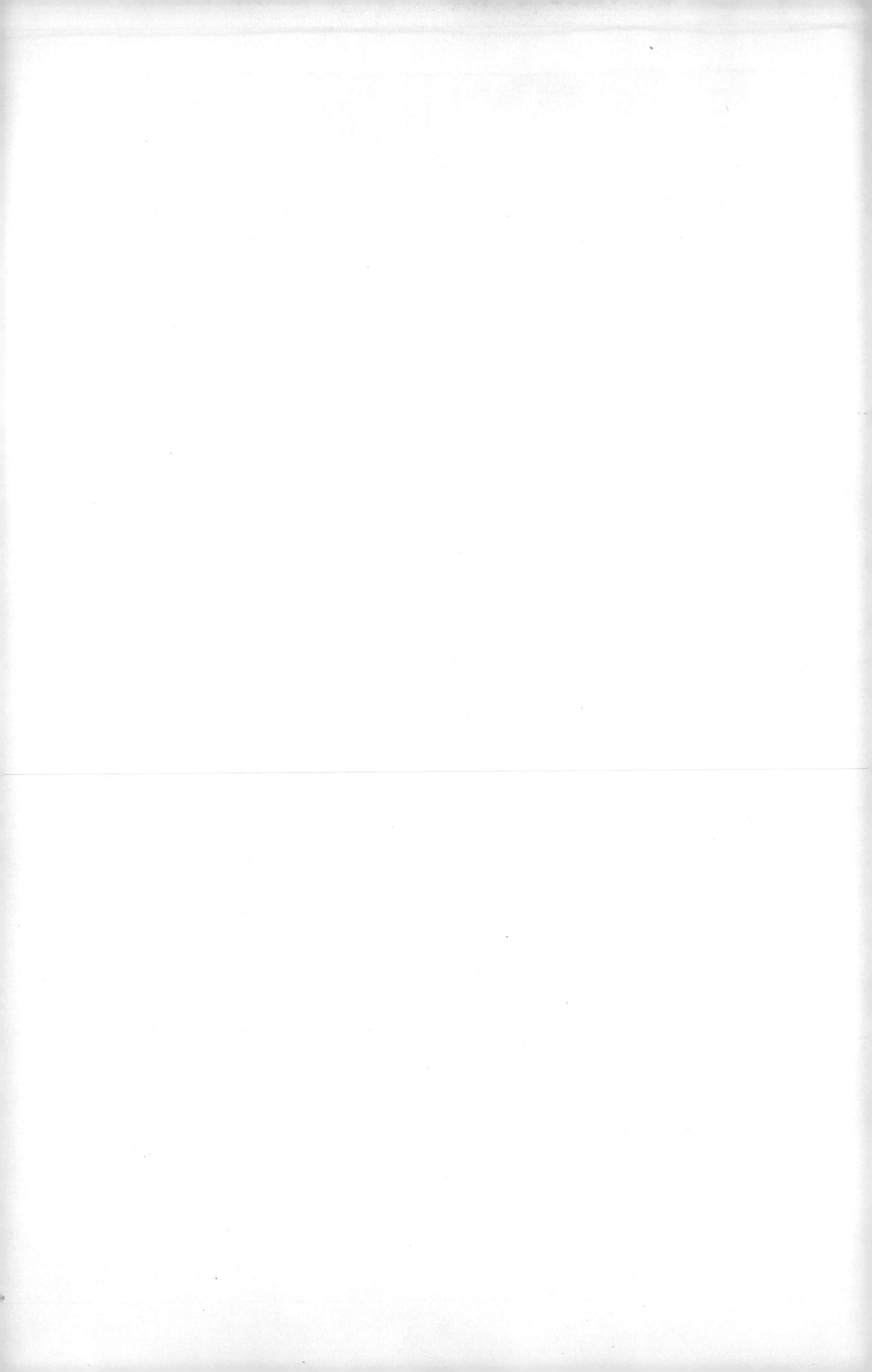

The Robot and the Sparrow
by Jake Parker 2004

ONCE THERE WAS A ROBOT. JETTISONED WITH THE REST OF THE WEEKS GARBAGE HE FELL SILENTLY TO THE GROUND. THERE HE DID SOMETHING HE HAD NEVER DONE BEFORE. HE RESTED.
WINTER FADED AND THE SUN ROSE EARLIER NOW. IT ALSO SET LATER EVERY EVENING.
fwap
fwap
?
HELLO?

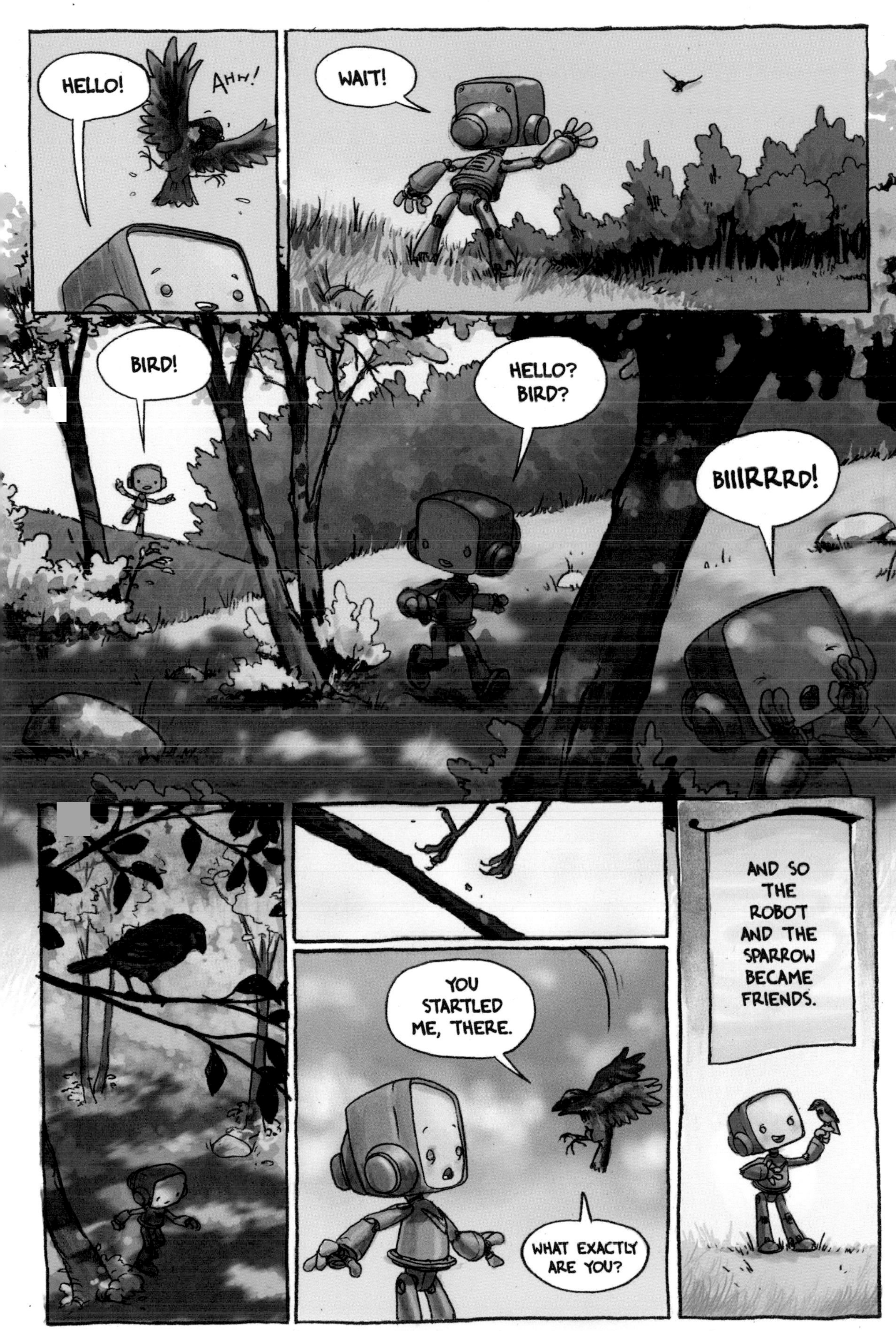
HELLO!
AHH!
WAIT!
BIRD!
HELLO? BIRD?
BIIIRRRD!
YOU STARTLED ME, THERE.
WHAT EXACTLY ARE YOU?
AND SO THE ROBOT AND THE SPARROW BECAME FRIENDS.

THE ROBOT HAD MANY QUESTIONS ABOUT SPARROW'S WORLD, SO THEIR DAYS WERE FILLED WITH EXPLORING AND DISCOVERY.
Z

WHAT DO ROBOTS DREAM ABOUT?
WHAT'S DREAM?
HMMM...
THOUGH THE SPARROW HAD A VERY CLEAR IDEA OF WHAT DREAMING WAS IN HIS OWN HEAD, HE FOUND IT WAS A VERY HARD THING TO EXPLAIN...
AT LENGTH THE SPARROW DECIDED THAT DREAMING WAS SOMETHING LEFT FOR THE BIRDS, AND DWELLED UPON IT NO MORE.

AS THE YEAR WORE ON THE SUN ROSE LATER IN THE MORNING AND SET EARLIER IN THE DAY. THE ROBOT WAS AMAZED AT HOW MUCH THE LANDSCAPE WAS CHANGING AROUND HIM.
SPARROW! WHAT'S HAPPENING TO ALL THE LEAVES?
THEY ARE OLD AND FALLING OFF THE TREES.
NEXT YEAR'S LEAVES ARE COMING AND NEED ROOM TO GROW.
SOON, THE TREES WILL BE BARE...
THE FLOWERS GONE...
AND THE INSECTS WILL HIDE THEMSELVES AWAY.
WINTER IS COMING.

ROBOT?

YES, SPARROW?

THE FIRST SNOW-FLAKE WILL SOON FALL. IT WILL BECOME TOO COLD FOR ME HERE.

ALL OF THE BIRDS FLY SOUTH TO WARM LANDS WHERE IT IS ALWAYS SUMMER AND WHERE THERE IS PLENTY TO EAT.
I CAN GO WITH YOU.

WHERE WE GO IS VERY FAR AWAY...

NOT EVEN LEGS AS STRONG AND QUICK AS YOURS CAN TAKE YOU THERE.

IT PAINED THE ROBOT TO HEAR THE SPARROW'S WORDS, BUT HE SOON CONCEDED. THEIR TIME WAS TOO SHORT TO BE STRAINED WITH WORRY.

Z
THE NIGHTS BECAME LONGER AND THE FOREST GREW COLD AND STILL.

THAT NIGHT, FOR THE FIRST TIME THE LITTLE ROBOT DREAMED.

the End

DEAD SOUL'S DAY OUT

A MALINKY ROBOT STORY

BY SONNY LIEW

ATARI & OLIVER
IN
DEAD SOUL'S DAY OUT
A MALINKY ROBOT STORY

"SHALL WE SING THE APPLE SONG? IF TWO PEOPLE SING IT'S MERRY.

IF EVERYONE SINGS, IT'S MORE AND MORE DELIGHTFUL.

LET'S PASS ON THE APPLE'S FEELINGS-

APPLE'S LOVEABLE, LOVEABLE'S THE APPLE"

-THE APPLE SONG (RINGO NO UTA) 1945

"*DIE!* OPTIMETRIX PRIME!"

HA HA!
DIE, OPTIMETRIX PRIME!!

PTUI! PTUI!
PTUI!

HEY GUYS!

ITS MISHA!
HEY MISHA!

OFF SCHOOL EARLY?
NO, NO IT'S A HOLIDAY TODAY.
PTUI! PTUI!

YOU SHOULDA COME EARLIER THEN! ME AND OLIVER WERE WATCHING MOVIES AT MR.ONO'S!

YEAH?
YEAH WE SAW THE TRANS-DEFORMERS MOVIE!
RAIN CLOUDS.

THAT'S A GOOD ONE.
THE BIG FIGHT AT THE END WAS BRILLIANT!
AND THAT SPACESHIP WITH THAT THING!

ANYHOW I WAS BUSY PACKING.
PACKING? EH?

I'M LEAVING FOR SANREO, REMEMBER?
WHAT?
THAT'S TODAY?

HMM...
FORGOT ALL 'BOUT THAT...

NO WORRIES...
HEY! I GOT YOU GUYS SOMETHING!

WHAT'S IT?!
HANG ON A MINUTE...

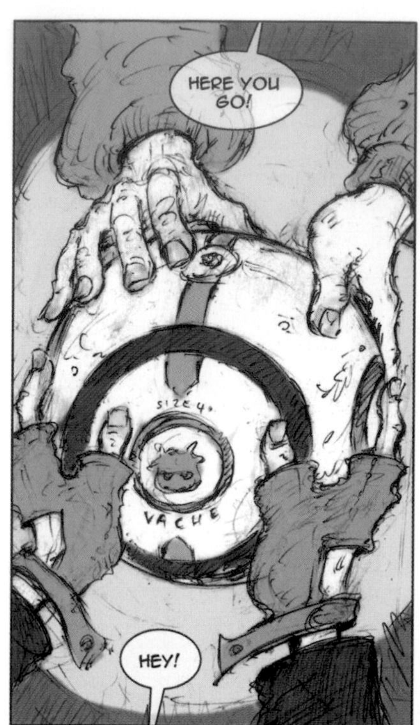
HERE YOU GO!
SIZE 4
VACHE
HEY!

CHECK IT OUT, OLIVER!
HA HA

THE *PSX-850!* THE LATEST ON THE MARKET!
IT'S BOO-TIFUL...

YOU WANNA PLAY A GAME, MISHA?
NAH...
HAFTA RUN, GOTTA HELP MY PARENTS PACK...

WHEN WILL YOU BE BACK?
FOR A VISIT?
DUNNO, A COUPLE OF MONTHS I GUESS...
I'LL SEND YOU GUYS A POSTCARD!

SEEYA MISHA!
SEEYA ATARI!

HOW BOUT YOU OLIVER?
UP FOR SOME FOOTIE?

OLIVER?

HEY.

A DAY...
...A DAY AMONGST FRIENDS.
MONEY IN YON POCKETS.

THE RAIN.
THE RAIN.

I LIKE IT LIKE THAT.
McDONNELL'S

REWARD!

$5,000

ROCO ROJO'S MONSTER IS STILL AT LARGE

ATTENTION ALL
SLAYERS

NOTE: MONSTER(S) MIGHT NOT LOOK LIKE DRAWINGS

THAT THING STINKS, MAN.

THEN TAKE IT OFF THE TABLE.

THE WAY YOU TACKLED THAT BEAST! MAN, I WAS AFRAID OF YOU!

HEY, EAT UP. YOU DON'T LOOK TOO GOOD.
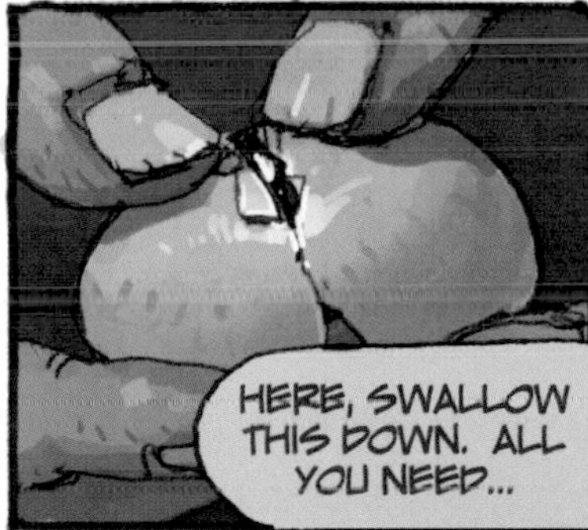
HERE, SWALLOW THIS DOWN. ALL YOU NEED...

...ARE A LITTLE NUTRIENTS!

THESE NOODLES... THEY TASTE OLD. AND THE SOUP LACKS FLAVOR. I SWEAR, ONE DAY I'LL HAVE MY OWN RESTAURANT AND-

YOU'LL QUIT THIS BUSINESS. I KNOW, I KNOW! WELL, A FEW MORE OF THESE BOUNTIES AND YOU JUST MIGHT SAVE ENOUGH MONEY FOR THAT DREAM OF YOURS.

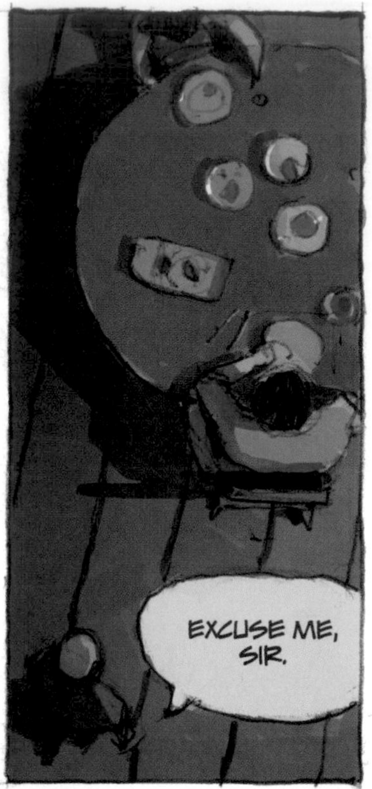

MONSTER SLAYERS

BY KHANG LE

NO WAY AM I RISKING MY LIFE FOR THAT SMALL REWARD!
ROCO ROJO? WHAT A DUMP! A DESERT TOWN FULL OF SAVAGES!

SOOO? HAHAHA! BUNCH OF CHEAPSKATES.
THOSE BEASTS JUST SEEM TO POP UP EVERYWHERE THESE DAYS.
THOSE POOR SOULS, DYING OF THIRST IS A HORRIBLE WAY TO GO.

EXCUSE ME SIR, I CAN'T GET CLOSE ENOUGH TO SEE. IS THAT THE NEW BOUNTY?
YES, IT'S JUST A SMALL REWARD FOR A BEAST DWELLING IN THE WELL OF ROCO ROJO. IT'S A DESERT TOWN SO THEY'RE DESPERATE FOR HELP. THAT MONSTER-

IS NO MATCH FOR ME! I WILL SLAUGHTER THAT FORSAKEN BEAST WITH MY BARE HANDS--
WHO'S THIS GUY

FOR I AM SIR AKIMA !!!

WHAT A LOSER.
HEY HEY! WHERE ARE YOU GOING? DON'T YOU WANT TO HEAR MY STORY ABOUT SLAYING THE BEAST OF AGAMORA?

RED PHOENIX
RESTAURANT

ZZZZZ

WAH!

2+2=4!

HAHAHA! SORRY MAN, YOU SHOULD HAVE SEEN YOUR FACE.
WHAT TOOK YOU SO LONG? WHAT TIME IS IT?
A BIT PAST NOON. HEY DID YOU SEE THAT NEW REWARD?

YEAH YEA...SO HOW MUCH DID WE GET FOR THAT HEAD?
UMM...IT WASN'T AS MUCH AS I HOPED FOR.

REMEMBER THAT WE ARE A DAY LATE ON THE KILL.
YEAH YEA...HOW MUCH?
350 $

350 ?!

AND THEY TAXED US FOR 120 SO IT'S ACTUALLY ONLY 230.

WELL...WE'RE LATE...AND THE DAMAGE COST. I COULDN'T BELIEVED HOW MUCH THOSE TWO BUDDHA STATUES WORTH...AND...

HEY I GOT YOU A HOT DOG!

THAT'S IT! YOU KNOW WHAT?...I QUIT.

RESTAURANT
I CAN'T STAND THIS RAIN.

I CAN'T STAND THIS HEAT.

HEY. WE GOT COMPANY.

COULD BE DESERT THIEVES. BE READY.

OH. THEY'RE JUST HEALERS.

WHERE ARE THESE INJURED PEOPLE COMING FROM?

THEY'RE SLAYERS FROM ROCO ROJO.
ARE THEY ALRIGHT?

THEY'RE DEAD.

TOC!
SNAP OUT OF IT, MAN!

CAW!
ROCO ROJO

WE'RE HERE.

CREEK!

VZZZZZ...

DAMN. I DIDN'T KNOW THE SITUATION WAS THIS BAD.

HELP US! *COUGH COUGH!* ... I'M SO THIRSTY.

SO, WHERE IS THE WELL THAT THIS BEAST DWELLS IN?

IT IS- *COUGH* ...STRAIGHT AHEAD, IN THE CENTER OF OUR TOWN.
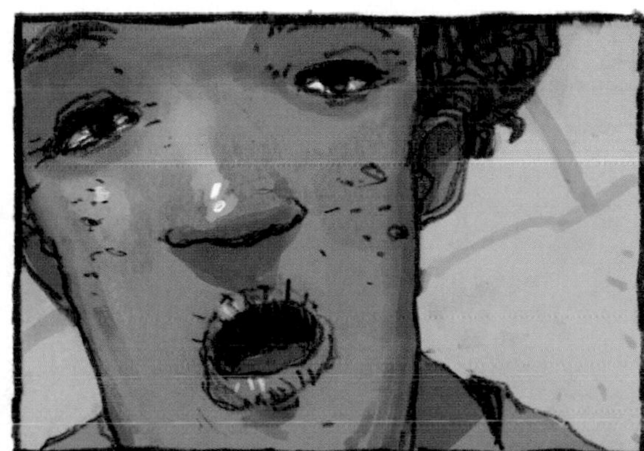

HERE, TAKE THIS. THERE'S NOT MUCH LEFT, BUT IT SHOULD HELP.
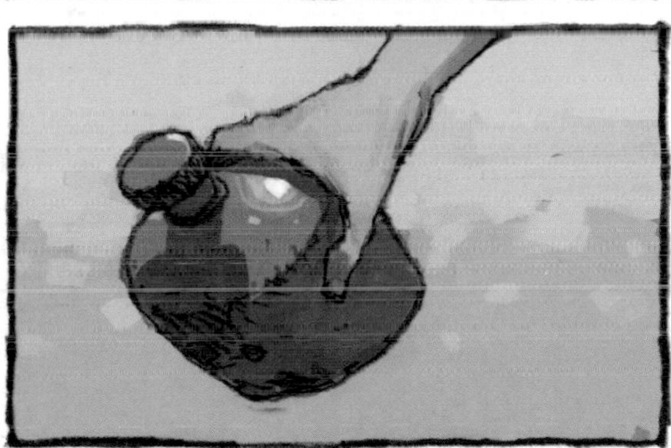

THAT WAS OUR WATER FOR THE JOURNEY BACK.
I KNOW. I GUESS WE'LL JUST HAVE TO GET RID OF THAT MONSTER AND REFILL OUR BOTTLES.

LETS GO MAKE SOME MONEY AND SAVE THE DAY.

SO WHERE IS THIS BEAST?

JUST IN TIME! THE LAST SLAYER HAS BEEN DOWN THERE FOR OVER AN HOUR, NOW.
DOESN'T LOOK LIKE HE'S GONNA COME UP ANYTIME SOON. WE'RE DESPERATE FOR HELP! THAT UNSEEN BEAST IS KEEPING US FROM OUR ONLY SOURCE OF WATER!
BUT BEWARE, SLAYERS. ALL WHO'VE DESCENDED NEVER RETURNED. ARE YOU SURE ABOUT THIS?

YOU SURE ABOUT THIS? 5000 IS REALLY NOT ENOUGH TO RISK OUR LIVES FOR.

BECAUSE OF OUR DESPERATE SITUATION, WE HAVE RAISED THE REWARD FROM 5000 TO...
CLIK!

85,000.

WHA! HOLD ON!
ZIP

JUST WAIT HERE FOR ME.

HEY HAO...

HOW DOES PHO LI CUISINE SOUND?

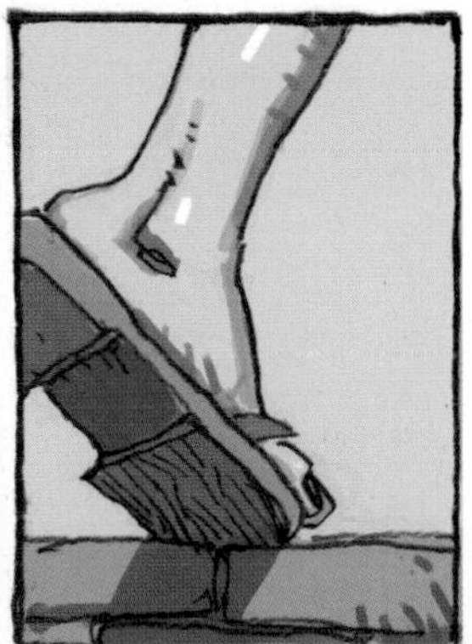

AARG
SPLASH!
LI!
HE'S A GONNER!
HE'S A GONNER!
HE'S A GONER!

LI!...

THIS IS HORRIBLE. HOW MANY MORE MUST DIE BEFORE WE ARE RID OF THIS MONSTER.
I'M SORRY FOR YOUR LOST SLAYER. YOU SHOULD GO HOME. HE'S A GONER! WE DON'T WANT TO WITNESS ANY MORE CASUALTIES TODAY.
HEY! WHAT ARE YOU DOING?

... I GOTTA GO.

LI!
LI!
I'M OVER HERE.
YOU'RE ALIVE! HOLD ON A SEC! LET ME LIGHT THE FLARE.

GRAA!!
CRAP.

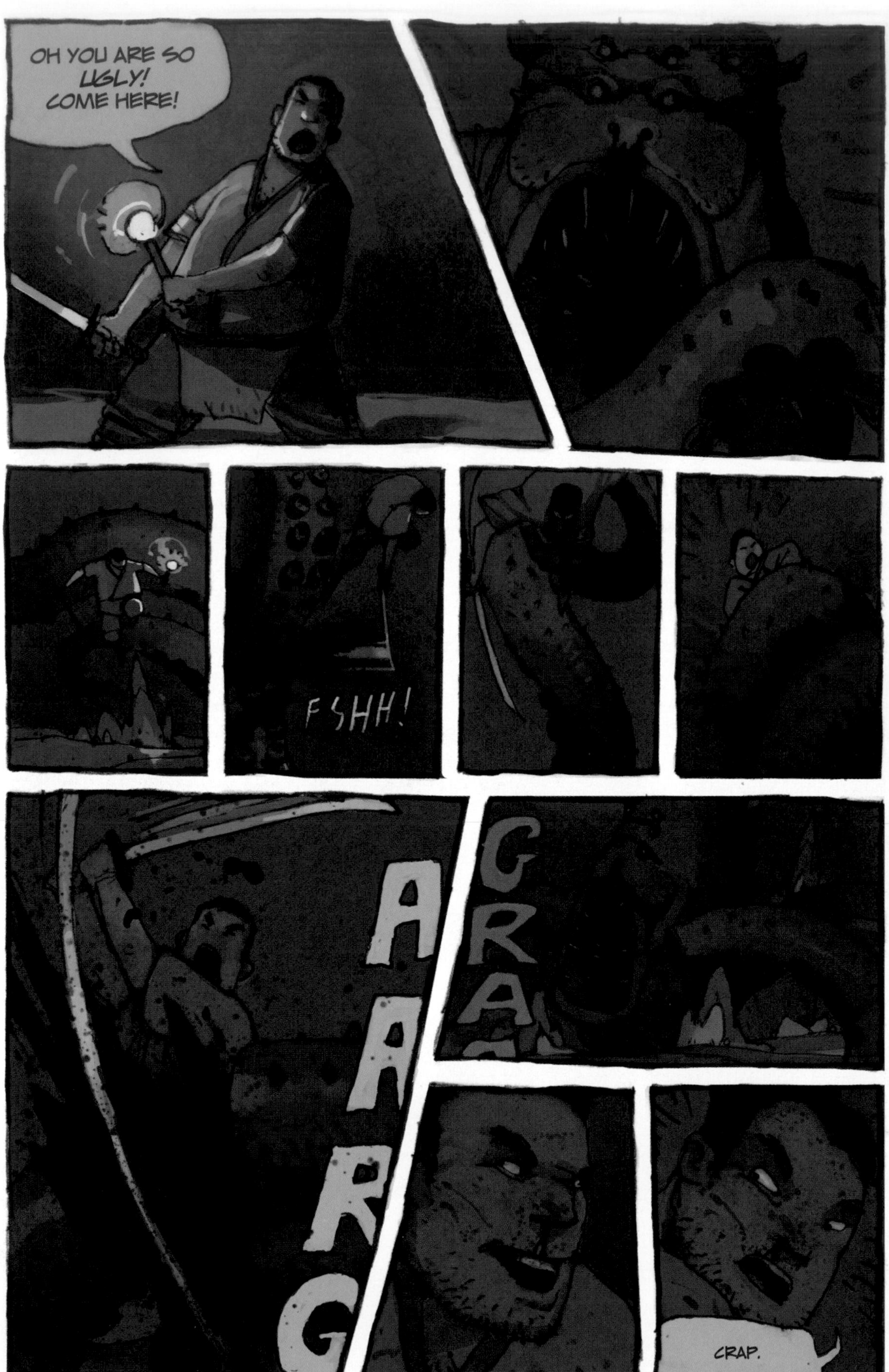

OH YOU ARE SO UGLY! COME HERE!
FSHH!
AAARG
GRAA
CRAP.

SMAK!

HAO!

WAKE UP HAO!

HAO!

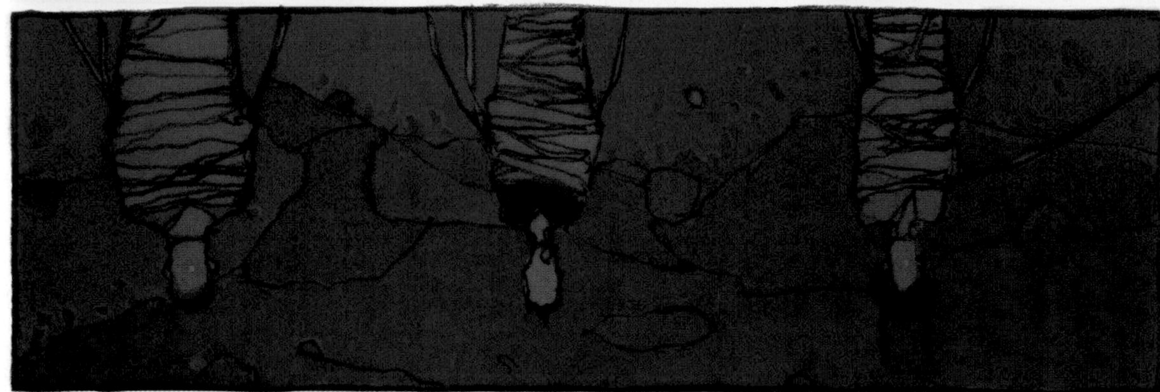

WUH?...WHA?...
WHERE ARE
WE?

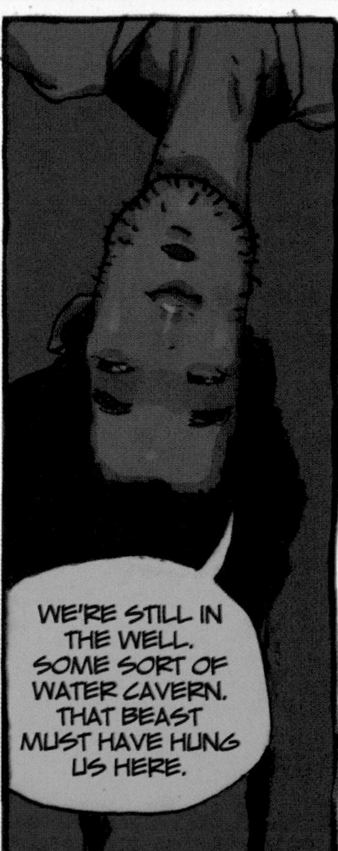
WE'RE STILL IN THE WELL. SOME SORT OF WATER CAVERN. THAT BEAST MUST HAVE HUNG US HERE.

AND IT'S POPPING OUT EGGS.

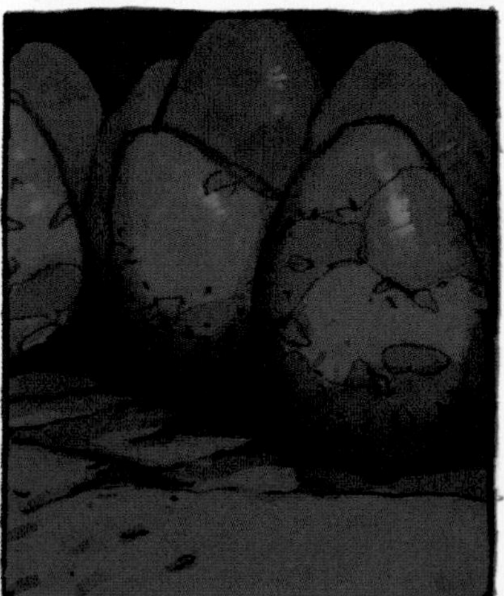

THAT'S ONE UGLY MOTHER. ...I WONDER WHY WE'RE STILL ALIVE?

GRAAC

PLOP!

NUTRIENTS.

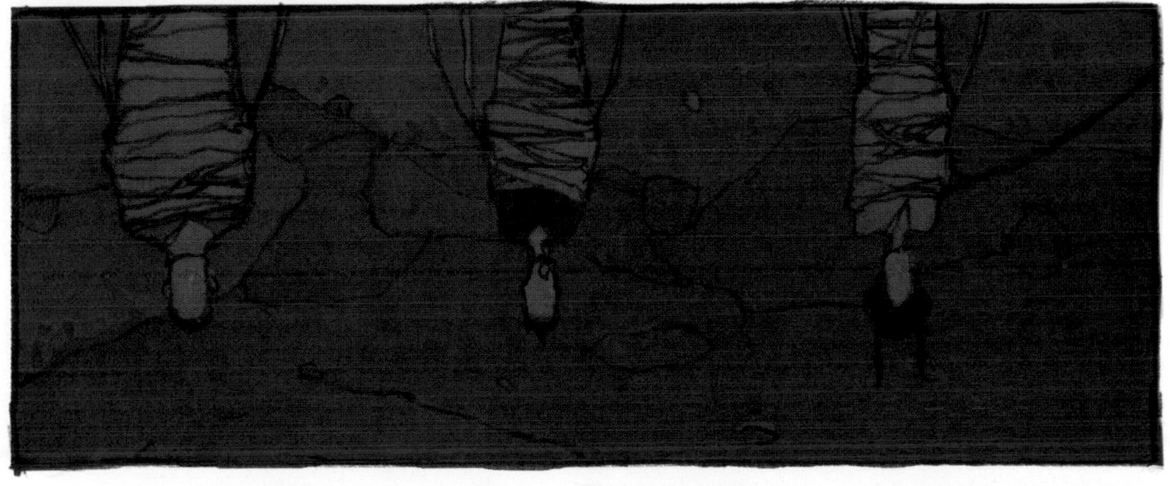

DAMN...
THIS SUCKS.

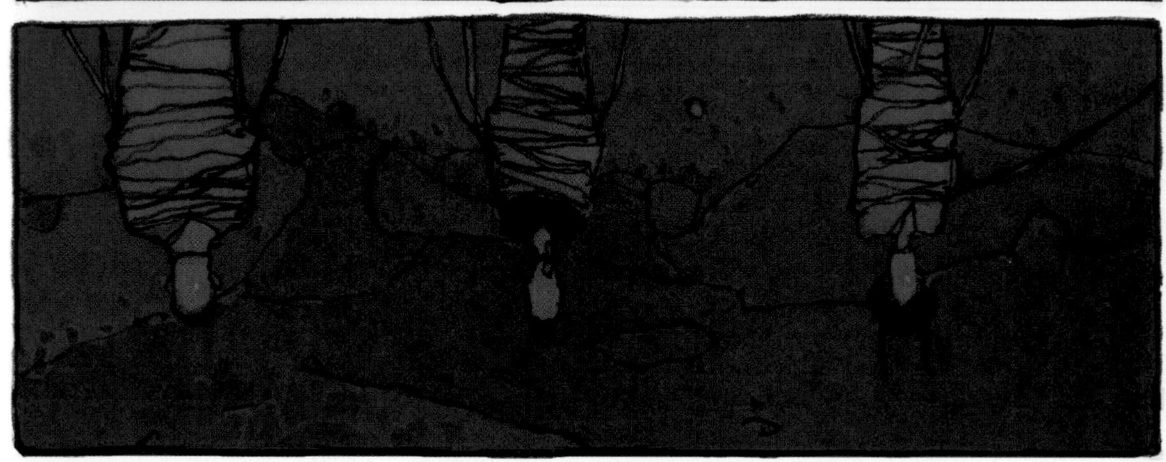

HEY LI? THERE'S SOMETHING I GOTTA CONFESS.

WHAT IS IT.

ABOUT THE LAST BOUNTY...WE ACTUALLY GOT MORE THAN 230.

ON THE WAY BACK...I KINDA STOPPED BY THE GOLDEN NUGGET CASINO.
WHAT? HOW MUCH DID YOU LOSE?
I WAS UP AT FIRST! ALMOST GOT ENOUGH FOR THAT RESTAURANT OF YOURS. THEN, I LOST ABOUT...2,600.

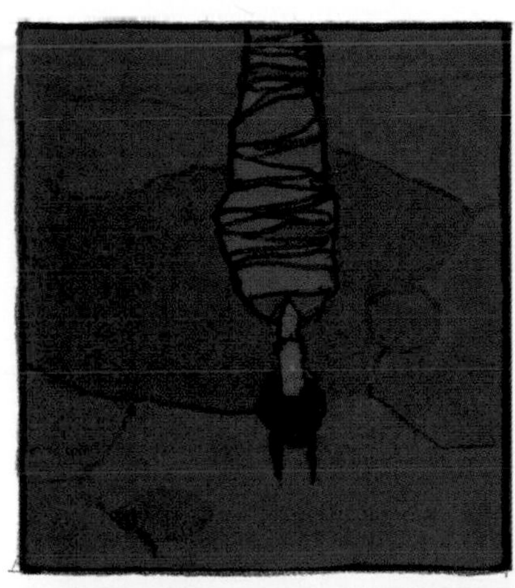

HEY, AREN'T YOU MAD?

NO...NOT REALLY.

NO?! BUT I PUT US IN THIS POSITION!
WELL IT DOESN'T MATTER NOW.
WE'RE GONNA END UP LIKE THIS GUY IN THE MIDDLE.
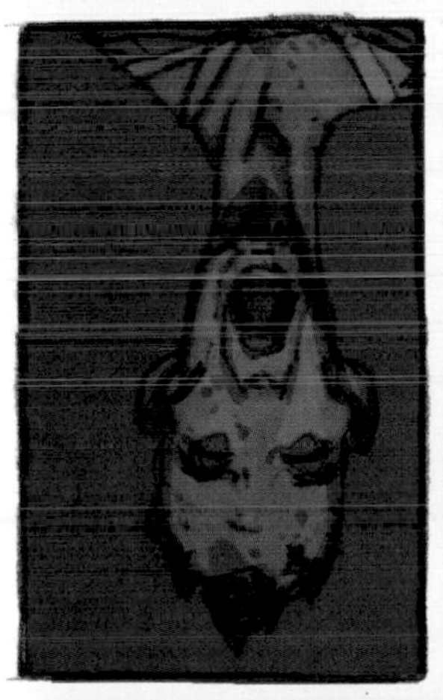
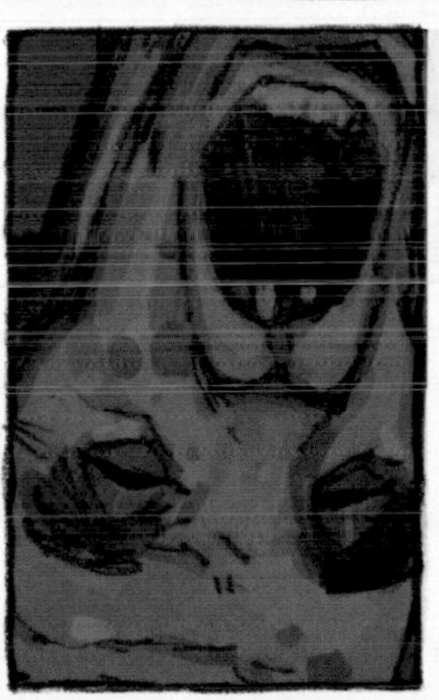

UGH... WHAT IS THAT?
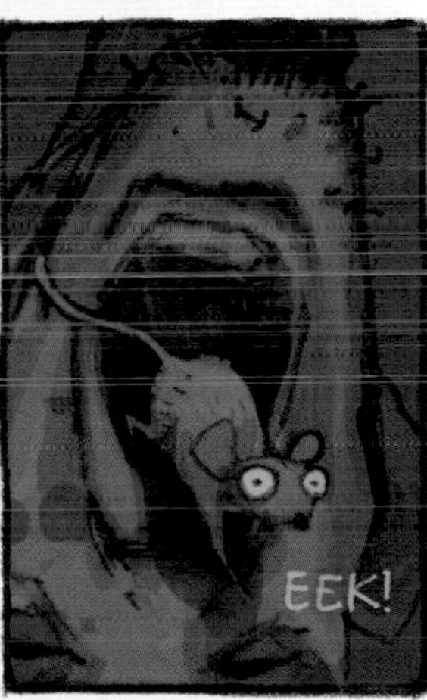
EEK!
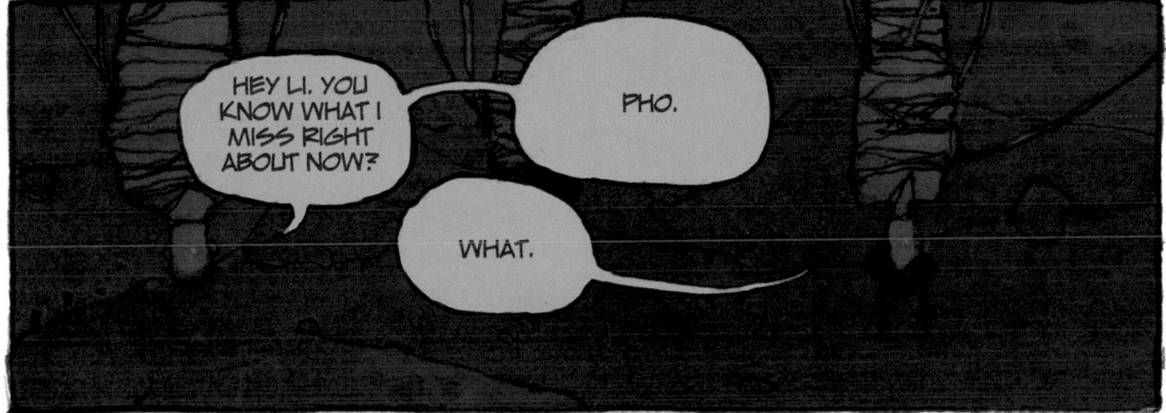
HEY LI. YOU KNOW WHAT I MISS RIGHT ABOUT NOW?
WHAT.
PHO.

MMM...THAT HOT STEAMY BROTH WITH THIN TENDER SLICES OF RARE BEEF...

...ADDING SOME BEAN SPROUTS AND MINT LEAVES...

...SOME HOT SAUCE AND HOISIN SAUCE FOR EXTRA FLAVOR ...

THEN A SQUEEZE OF LIME TO TOP IT OFF. DAMN LI...I'M SALIVATING...

HOW ABOUT YOU MAN...WHAT DO YOU MISS MOST FROM THIS WORLD?

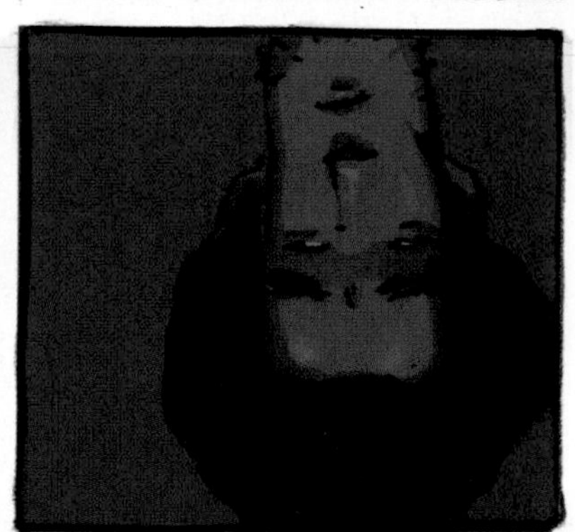

...I DON'T KNOW.

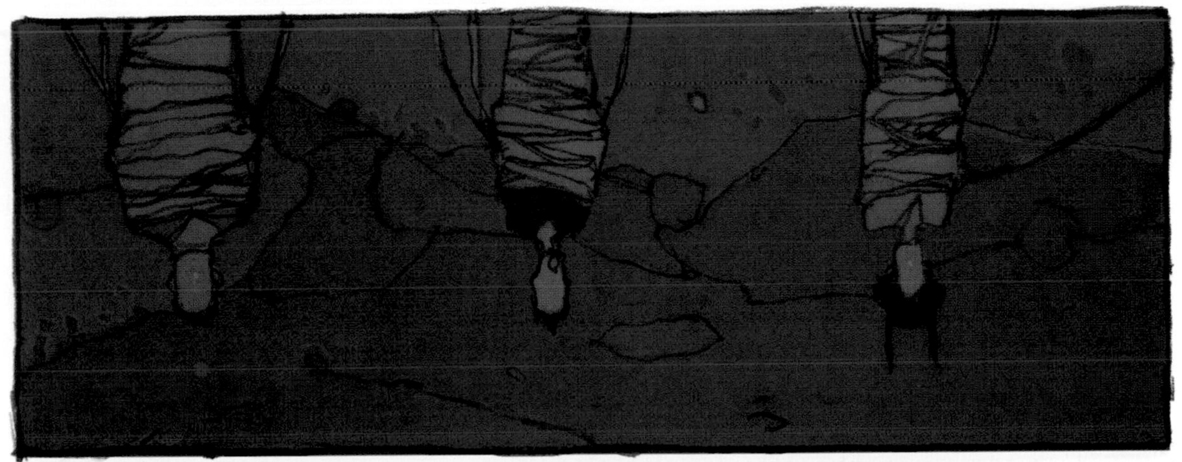

WELL...IF THIS IS THE END, I GUESS WE'RE STILL IN IT TOGETHER HUH.
HEY LI?... WHAT IS THIS UGLY MOTHER ANYWAY?
I DON'T KNOW. IT LOOKS KIND OF FAMILIAR. I MUST HAVE SEEN IT FROM A MUSEUM OR SOMETHING. I RECOGNIZE CERTAIN FEATURES...

THE RED LEATHERY SKIN, AND THE SPIKES ON THE TENTACLES.

AND THAT TUNNELING MOUTH OF TEETH. AND THOSE SIX RED EYES...THOSE RED GLOWING EYES...WAIT A MINUTE...

THAT BUTTERLY PATTERN ON THE BACK! HAHAHA...*I CAN'T BELIEVE THIS!* WHY DIDN'T I RECOGNIZE IT BEFORE?!

HAHAHAHA!
AND THOSE SQUID-LIKE *SUCTION CUPS!* HAHAHA! NO WAY! HAHA...COUGH!.. ***HAHAHA!***

EHEHEH...WHAT SO FUNNY?
YOU WON'T BELIEVE THIS MAN! AHAHAha...COUGH!.. AHA...OW. MY RIBS HURT...

AHA...AHAH AHAHHAHA HAHAHA!

WHAT IS IT LI?!

AHAHAHA!

WHAT THE HELL IS SO FUNNY?!!!

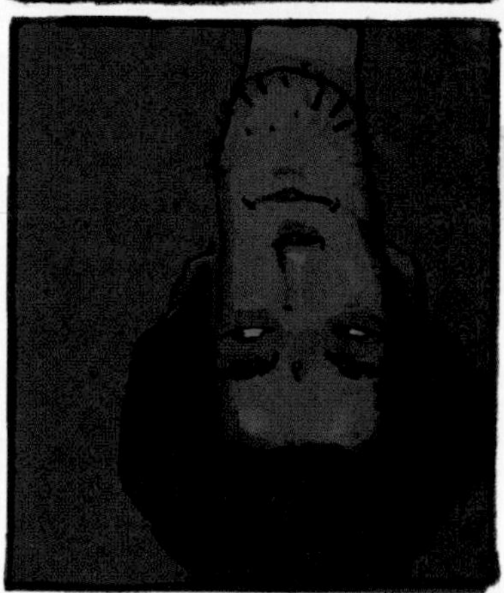

WE'RE NOT GONNA DIE HERE.

THE NAME OF THIS MONSTROSITY IS *DAIGONO.*

U MEAN ALL WE HAVE TO DO IS JUST WAIT?!

THIS IS GREAT! SO WE'RE NOT GONNA DIE!

YUP. JUST PATIENCE. HEHEH... NO WONDER THIS BEAST WAS SO HOSTILE. IT ONLY HAS ONE CHANCE TO GIVE LIFE.

NOT ONLY THAT. ONCE THE DAIGONO IS DEAD, WE'LL JUST COME UP AND CLAIM THE REWARD!

I CAN FINALLY OPEN MY RESTAURANT! ISN'T THIS GREAT! AHAHAHA!

AHAHAH! PHO LI CUISINE! I LIKE THE SOUND OF THAT! AHAHAHHA!

GRAOOO
OK, I THINK THIS IS IT!

GRAARAOOOOooo
THREE!

PLOP!
TWO!

ONE!

PHO LI CUISINE!

WE'RE RICH!

I KNOW! ISN'T THIIS GREAT! I WOULD HAVE TO SAY THIS IS BY FAR THE EASIEST AND MOST PROFITABLE BOUNTY WE EVER GOT.
ACTUALLY... HEHEHE...WE DIDN'T REALLY DO ANYTHING! AHAHAHA!

AHA! THAT'S RIGHT! ALL WE DID WAS HANG AROUND! AHAHAHA! I SAID "HANG"! AHAHAHAHA!

EHE...HEH...HEY LI. NOW WHAT DO WE DO?

HMM...LET ME THINK FOR A SEC. MAYBE I CAN TWITCH MY WAY OUT OF THIS...

SPLASH

WHAT WAS THAT?!

HELLO! IS SOMEONE THERE?

DO NOT FEAR CAPTURED SLAYERS! YOUR SAVIOR HAS COME!

NOOO...

FOR I AM SIR. AKIMA! AND I HAVE SLAYED THE BEAST OF AGAMORA!!!

I AM IN LUCK TODAY. THE FILTHY BEAST IS ASLEEP. IT WILL BE AN EASY KILL!
NOW PLEASE STAY QUIET. I MUST APROACH IT WITH A SUPRISE ATTACK.
BUT THE BEAST IS ALREADY...
AARG!...
AARG!...
AAARGH
NOOOOO!...

THANK YOU ALL! MY NAME IS SIR. AKIMA! AND I AM JUST A SIMPLE MAN.

LOOK AT HIM. HE REALLY THINKS HE SAVED THE DAY.
C'MON, LET'S GO.

HEY, THANKS FOR COMING DOWN AFTER ME.

WELL AT LEAST THIS TOWN SEEMS MUCH LIVELIER. SO WHERE ARE WE HEADING?
TO THE OCEAN.

SO WHAT ARE WE DOING HERE?

I KINDA STOLE SOME LITTLE SOUVENIRS FROM ROCO ROJO.

YOU'RE CRAZY! WHAT ARE YOU GONNA DO WITH THOSE?

JUST PUTTING THEM BACK WHERE THEY BELONG.

YOU ALMOST FINISHED DOWN THERE? I'M STARVING MAN.
JUST A SECOND. GOTTA FIND A GOOD SPOT.

ALRIGHT. LET'S GET OUT OF HERE.

YEAH...I FELT KIND OF BAD FOR THAT UGLY MOTHER TOO.

YEAH...SAME HERE. THAT'S WHY I DECIDED TO SAVED THE TWO EGGS.

TWO? I THOUGHT I SAW THREE EGGS IN THE SACK. WHAT HAPPENED TO THE THIRD ONE?

DINNER!

AHAHAHA! YOU BAD! I NEVER HAD MONSTER'S EGG BEFORE, WONDER WHAT IT'LL TASTE LIKE.
I GUESS WE'LL FIND OUT. AHEM...SOOO...YOU LOST 2,600 AT THE GOLDEN NUGGET?..
I'M TELLING YOU LI! I WAS UP LIKE 13,000! IT WAS ALMOST ENOUGH FOR YOUR RESTAURANT AND...
YEAH...YEA... WHATEVER MAN. THAT'S THE LAST TIME I LET YOU GO COLLECT THE BOUNTY.

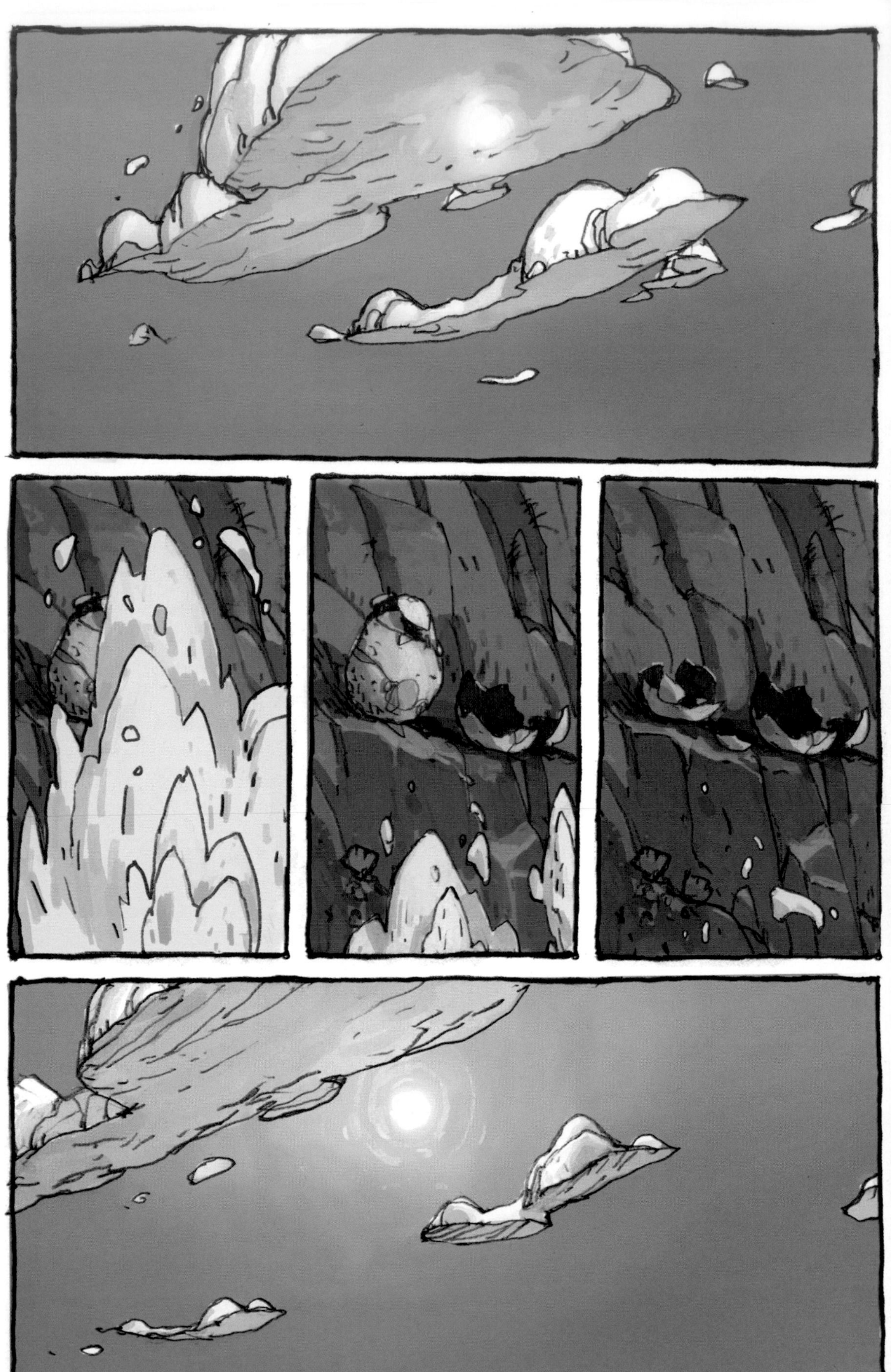

the end.

The Golden Temple

continued from "Taj Mahal," Flight Volume One

Written & Illustrated by

Neil Babra

I used to live here when I was a kid.

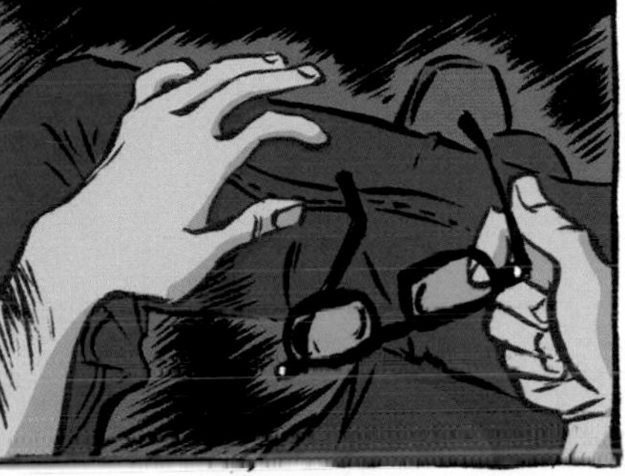

I had a precocious command of the languages, according to my father.

Sometime after we left, I forgot.

But there were a few words that stayed.

"Pani" somehow sounds more real in my mind than the English translation: "water."

I think of the sound, like it's an onomatopoeia.

And I remember splashing around in a monsoon...

...Just one second before it ended.

It's hard to explain how a casual word could feel like, a secret...

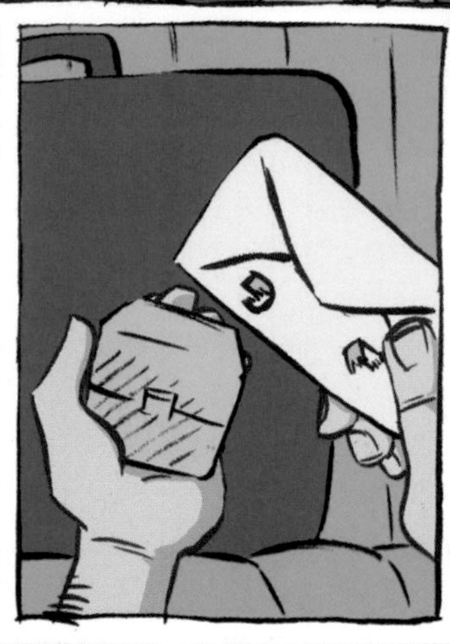

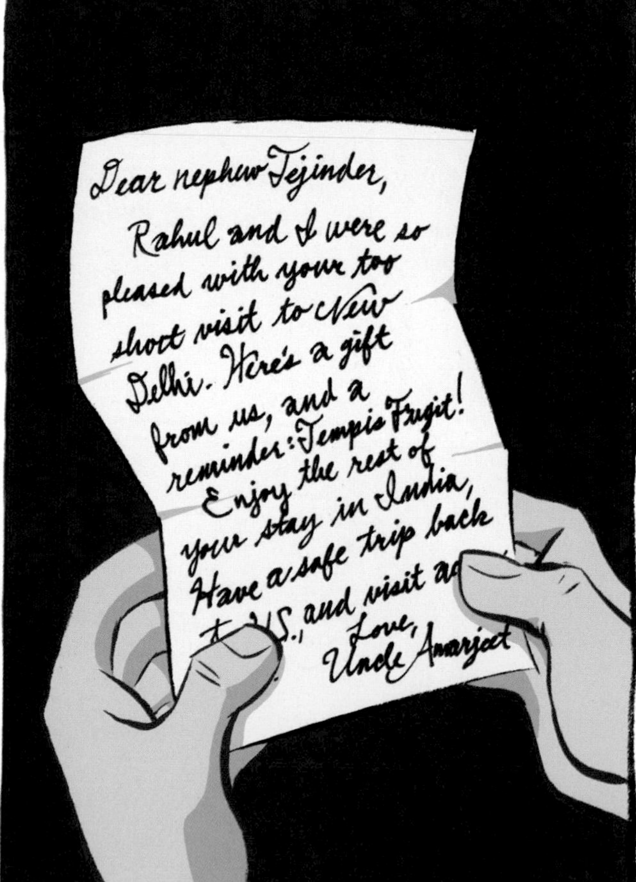

Dear nephew Tejinder,

Rahul and I were so pleased with your too short visit to New Delhi. Here's a gift from us, and a reminder: Tempis Fugit! Enjoy the rest of your stay in India, Have a safe trip back to U.S., and visit ag

Love,
Uncle Amarjeet

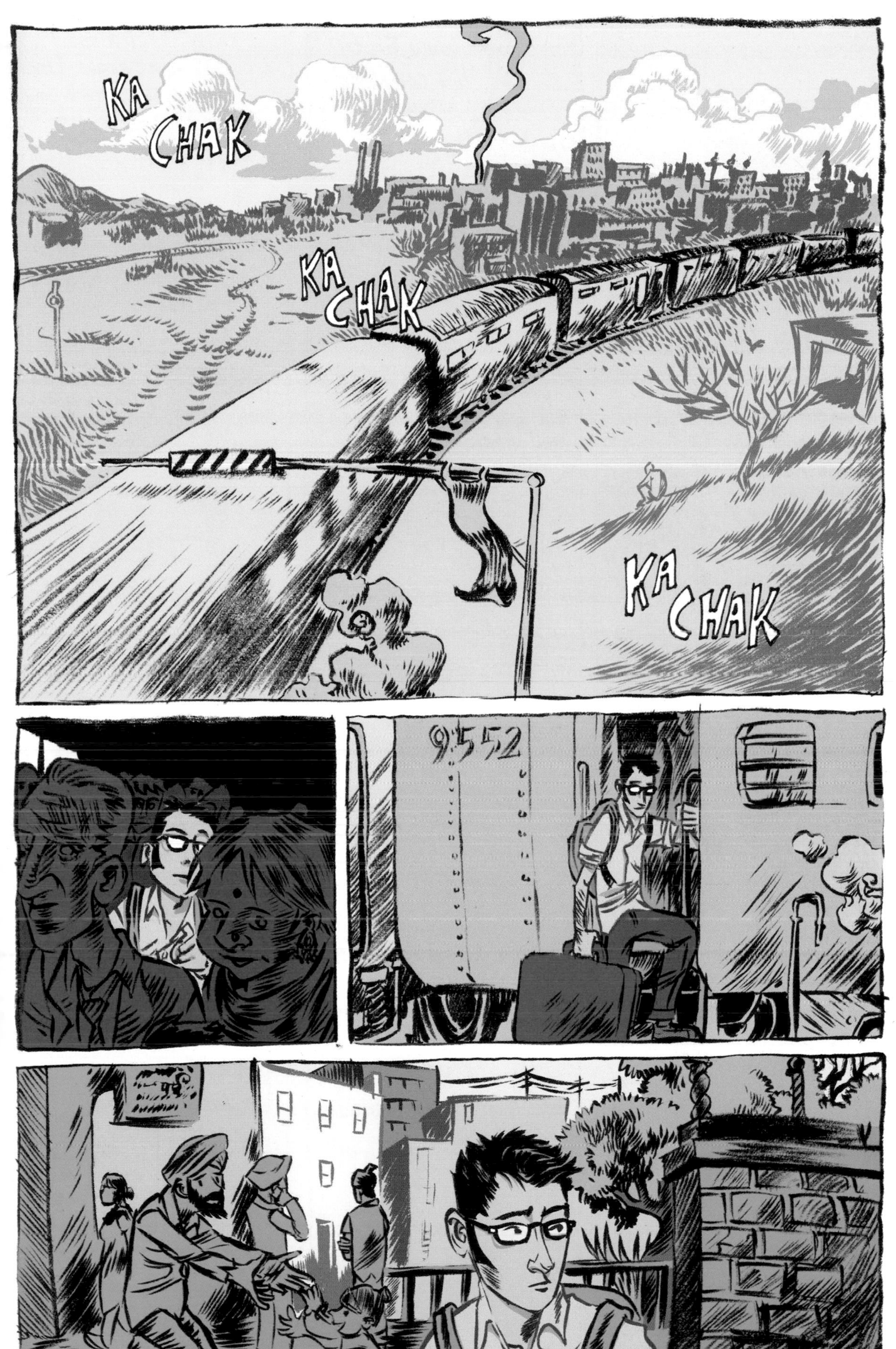
KA CHAK
KA CHAK
KA CHAK
9552

Tej?!

Wow, Bitty? You completely grew up!

I also outgrew that name, but your family won't listen!

Hah, Neha!
Oh, is my aunt here? They said she'd pick me up...

Well, I thought I'd give her a chance to clean up before you came!

Heh, heh.
She can't waste any time.

We should get a car; I just walked here.
Oh...

...I don't mind walking if you don't.
I've been sitting in a train for hours, and it's such a nice day...

It's probably snowing back in Pittsburgh right now!
But, your bags?

No no, I packed light, see?

If you insist! It's this way.

Comb, comb

Hey this looks pretty.
We can see the monument if you like.

Is this familiar to you?
I know it's really weird, but I don't remember much at all.
APRIL 1919

DEDICATED
MASSACRE OF
DS OF INNO-
NDUS, SIKHS,
LIMS AT THE
OF TROUPS
DED BY THE
BRITISH ARMY.
YER
No... That must have been, Sixteen years ago?

Things here must seem strange, having grown up abroad.
A little, but it's interesting. Have you read any Edward Said? Sometimes an exile has the best perspective.

An exile?

In a manner of Speaking.

WHERE THE
BULLET HOLES
ARE STILL VISI
IN THE PARK WA
But you're an American!

...Hey, my dad's going to have a fit if I don't take more pictures.

Leave it to me.
Oh, nice camera!

Perfect!

So you had a nice time with Bitty?
Yeah, she's really nice.

You can meet her family tomorrow!

Thanks, Uncle.
Tej, your papa said there were no gurdwaras where you grew up?
Yeah, so we were never very religious. I think he feels guilty about that sometimes.

In the morning we'll visit Harimandir Sahib, the holiest shrine in India. Maybe it will mean something new, now that you're older.

Hey, is that real gold it's covered in?
...
Yes.

FWUMP.

knock.

Hi Auntie.
Good morning! Guess who's here to see you!
kexp

Sigh.
kexp

Rahul!

Hi again, Tej!
Wha, how did you get here?
I thought I missed you in New Delhi!

Well, I have to travel for this job, so I thought I'd pay you a visit while I can!

I'll get you boys something to cover your heads.
We have to go soon!

Are you feeling okay? My dad said you got the "Delhi Belly."
Much better, thanks.

Have you seen the view from their roof?
Not yet...

Thanks for the watch, by the way.
You're welcome! I have another gift here, if I can find it. We can share it.
kexp
Uh, that's a "bidi" right?
A hand-rolled cigarette?
Sure.
So, I'm kind of surprised you came anyway. We didn't get to talk much in New Delhi.
kexp
That's true. I think it was harder because I hadn't seen you in so long.
That makes sense. I'm basically a stranger here.
Are you sure you feel better?
Cough!
I don't know. I always felt like I left behind something important here.
But now I feel like...

...A tourist.

I guess I should have expected that. I wasn't even sure I'd remember what I was looking for.

Ah, I understand now...

Did you see the photo in your room in Delhi?

Of course... Your mother.

Sometimes I feel that I remember her but...
Not quite.

Despite that, I miss her very much.

Hey, Rahul..

There's nothing I can do about that, but...
I hope she'd be proud of me.
I think it must be a similar feeling.
I don't know how I'm ever gonna make my parents proud though.
I don't know what things will be like after I graduate.
And now I guess they want to arrange a marriage!
If you want to go into hiding, Pakistan is only 20km that way!
Well if it worked for Bin Laden...
Hey! Did you and your dad know about that?
I think they want to see if you like her.
They just want you to be happy.
As we all do.
Heh.
flick.

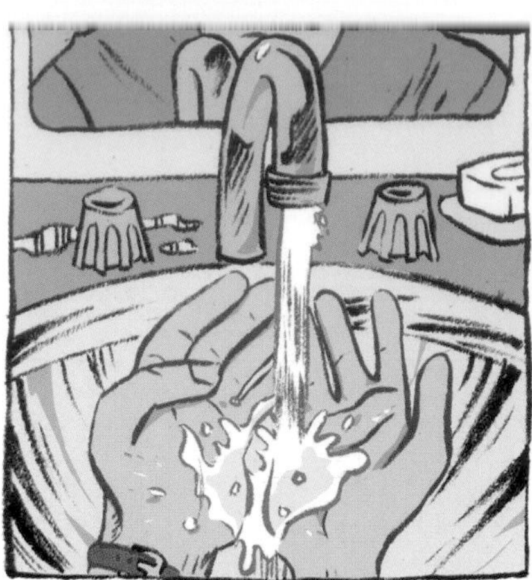

Stop it you loser!

Do we have enough umbrellas? It looks like it's going to rain.
Don't worry.

clack.

"DANCE OF the SUGAR PLUMS"

OR, LAST MONTH ON EARTH

BY DON HERTZFELDT

POPULAR SHRILL MUSIC PIPED IN FROM NEARBY RESTAURANT

AN ASTEROID HURTLES THROUGH DARKNESS. IT IS TOO EARLY TO TELL WHETHER IT WILL STRIKE THE PLANET.

HE PLOTS A VULGAR CRIME AS THE CHILDREN PLAY WITH THEIR SQUID.

THEY EAT TOFFEES, ALL THE WHILE UNSUSPECTING.

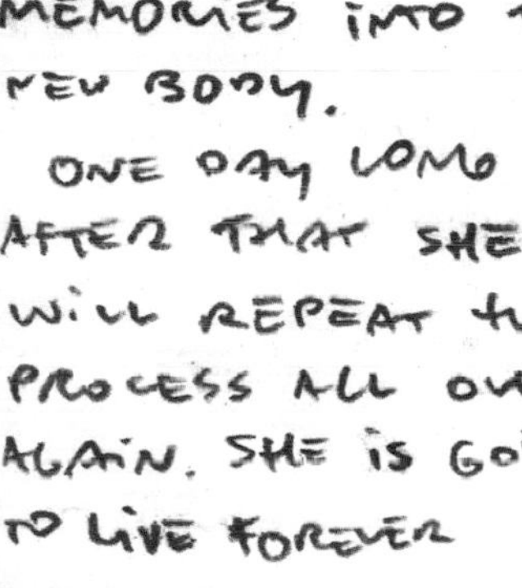
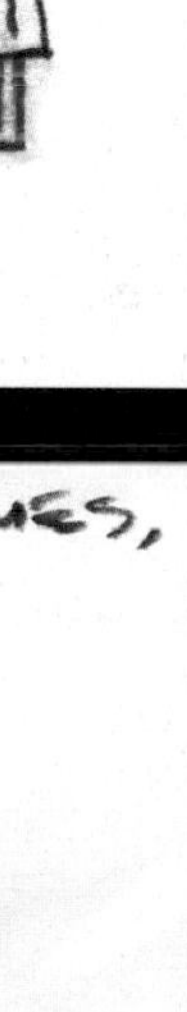
SCIENTISTS HAVE IMPREGNATED HER WITH A PERFECT CLONE OF HERSELF. ONE DAY SHE WILL UPLOAD ALL OF HER MEMORIES INTO THIS HEALTHY NEW BODY.
ONE DAY LONG AFTER THAT SHE WILL REPEAT THE PROCESS ALL OVER AGAIN. SHE IS GOING TO LIVE FOREVER

MANFISH MISLEADS THE PRINCESS, SENDING HER IN THE WRONG DIRECTION.

THE SEARCH CONTINUES, TO NO AVAIL

IT IS CERTAIN NOW. THE ASTEROID IS ON A COLLISION COURSE AND WILL MOST CERTAINLY FUCK EVERYTHING UP.

NATIONWIDE GOING OUT OF BUSINESS SALES

ANOTHER AGING ROCK STAR BECOMES A FADING PARODY OF REBELLION.

SOMETHING MAKES REPEATED SWOOPS OVER THEIR HEADS BEFORE ASCENDING INTO THE EVENING SKY.

THE WIND STIRS THE DEAD BIRD'S FEATHERS, SORT OF MAKING IT LOOK LIKE IT WAS JUST HAVING A BAD DREAM.

LAST CHANCE TO PURCHASE GLAMOROUS BOOTS AND HATS

A FRINGE GROUP GENERATES GOOD WILL.

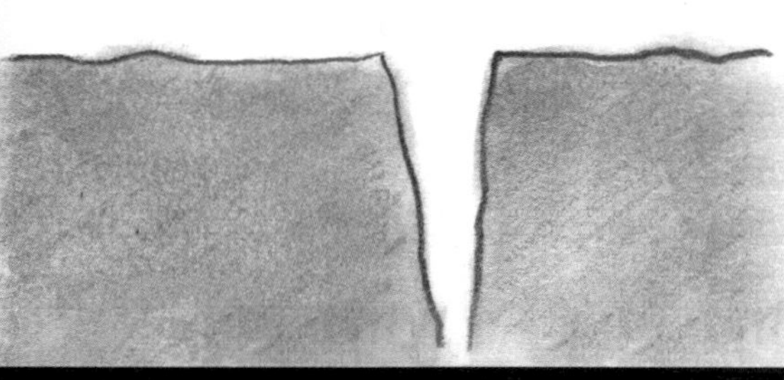

the PRINCESS DISAPPEARS INTO A CREVASSE.

IT'S ALL FUN AND GAMES UNTIL SOMEBODY GETS HURT, HE SAYS, SOME AQUATIC CREATURE STUCK TO HIS FACE.

ETHNIC CHILDREN AND SMALL BIRDS STARVE THEMSELVES AND DART AROUND the ROOM

the SUN SETS FOR TWO MONTHS.

SUSAN "COLLECTS THEM ALL"!

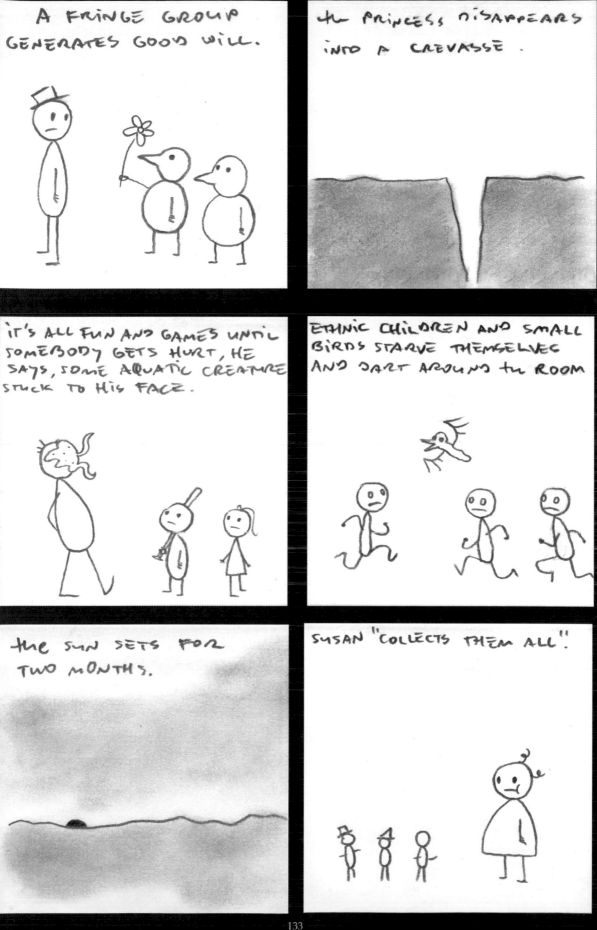

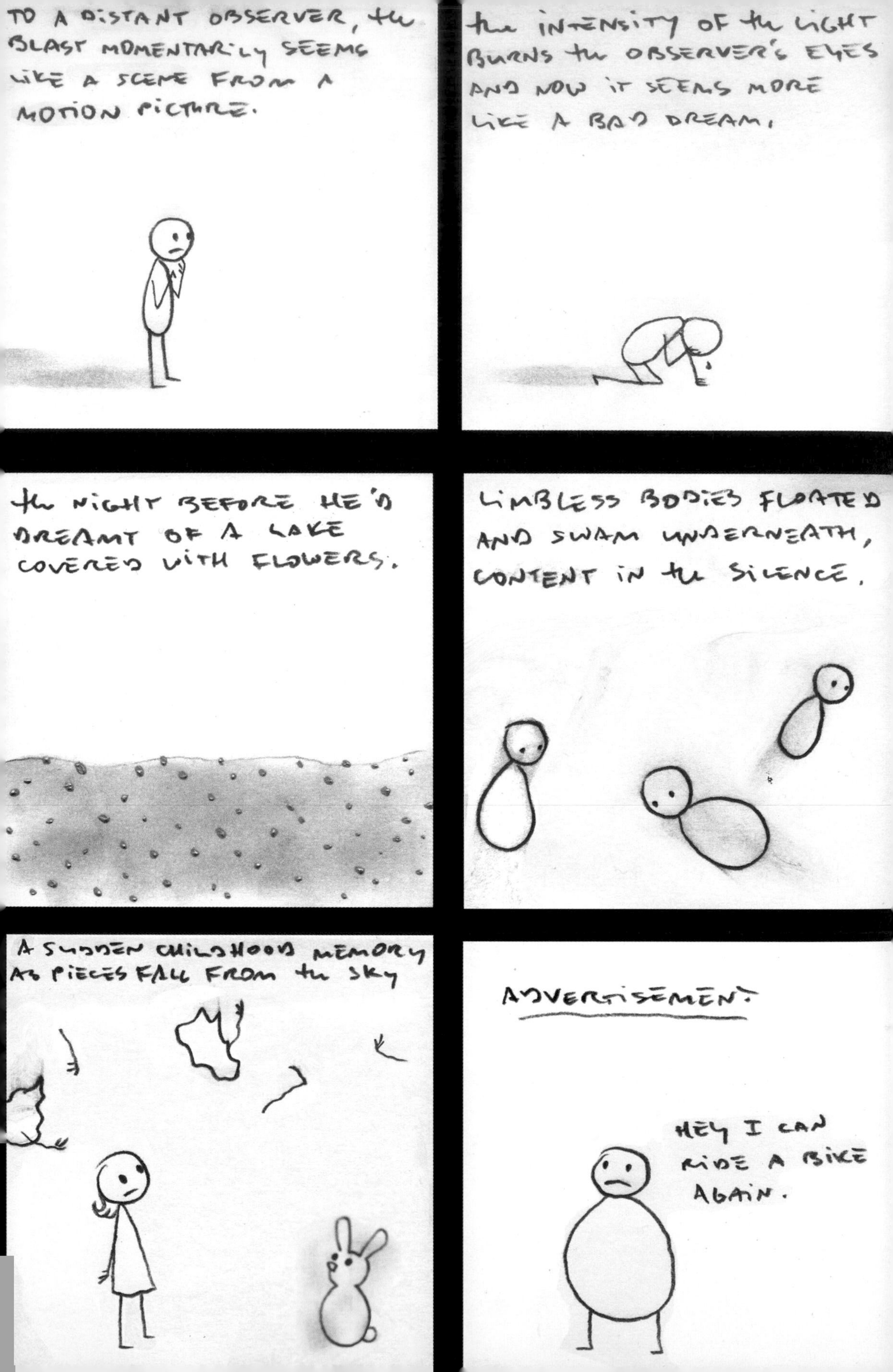
TO A DISTANT OBSERVER, THE BLAST MOMENTARILY SEEMS LIKE A SCENE FROM A MOTION PICTURE.
THE INTENSITY OF THE LIGHT BURNS THE OBSERVER'S EYES AND NOW IT SEEMS MORE LIKE A BAD DREAM.
THE NIGHT BEFORE HE'D DREAMT OF A LAKE COVERED WITH FLOWERS.
LIMBLESS BODIES FLOATED AND SWAM UNDERNEATH, CONTENT IN THE SILENCE.
A SUDDEN CHILDHOOD MEMORY AS PIECES FALL FROM THE SKY
ADVERTISEMENT:
HEY I CAN RIDE A BIKE AGAIN.

HIDING IN HOMES AND SAYING GOOD BYE

CARTOON MARATHON ON TELEVISION.

A PLASTIC BAG RATTLES ON THE END OF A BROKEN POLE

MASS CRUSTACEAN SUICIDES

DID SHE FORGET TO WATER THE CACTUS?

SOMEBODY LOST A BUTTON.

Destiny Express
traveling from
One stage of life, to the Next
Admit One
General Ticket Agent,
Jen Wang
94103

all aboard, children!
choo choo choo
choo choo
. . .

Resting between stages is not unheard of, but several days! May I ask, why?

Why not?

Well... there aren't many reasons to. We don't think when we pass from one stage of life to the next. It's merely a routine. There's no point in resting because it only stalls the process. In fact, most people anticipate the continuation of their journey. So I must admit, my dear, your lengthy stay has me a little worried.

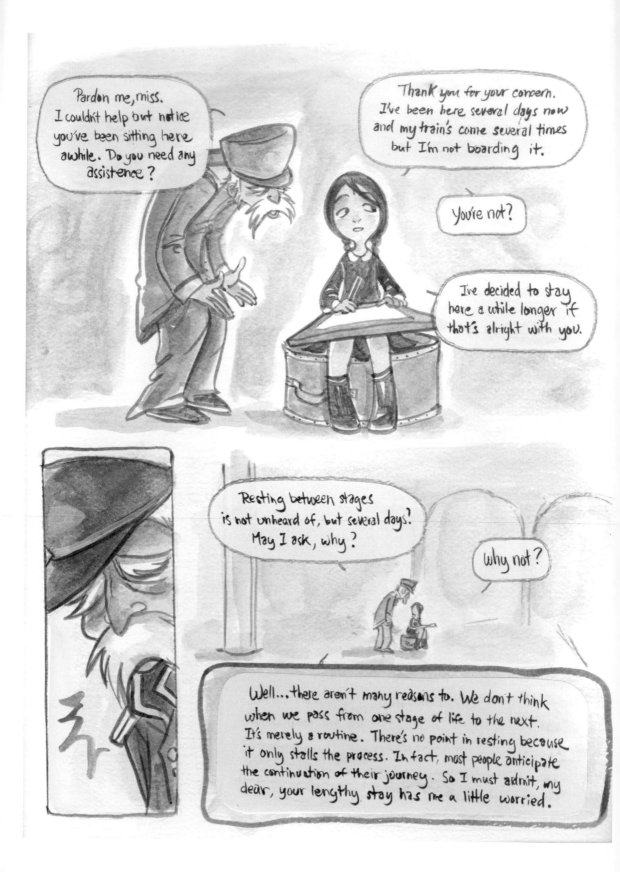

Well I'm stalling. Believe me sir, I was as excited as anybody when I boarded my last train here. It should take me into the new school year where I shall begin painting lessons.
But I've learned some news and I'm afraid I can't go on any further.
What sort of news?
. . .
Bad news.

On my way here I sat across from a fortune teller. She enjoyed my drawing very much and asked for a portrait of herself in exchange for a reading. I obliged innocently, not realizing the consequences of learning one's fate on a destiny train. She said only this to me:
In the next stage of your life, you will make a mistake.
A mistake so grave it could alter your experience of the world.

While her reading left me perplexed, I would not have considered staying if I hadn't noticed the two gentlemen waiting with me on the transfer station.

One man stood tall and pert, not a sign of misfortune upon his attractive form. His manner was clumsy, but he blushed and hummed to himself with a sincerity only reserved for the happiest children...

The other wore an expression of weariness, bundles of rugged scarves barely concealing the years of injustice and cynicism imprinted on his face. He moved very little, but when he did, he manuevered with a grace only possible through long-term exertion.

The two couldn't have been very far in age but their souls told a story generations apart

It was seeing them that trigged my decision to stay.

Fortune tellers can never be trusted, my dear.
As with anyone else who claims to gain knowledge from tea leaves and turtle shells.
But you must understand. I stay because I cannot risk the nature of my ART.
My innocence makes it beautiful. I see the world in stars and kalediscopes because I believe in the good of humanity.
Artistic possibilities are limited only by my imagination, and there are no horrible realities to taint it.

I'm afraid
if I make a mistake,
I will lose that
beauty...
...and my art
will forever be framed
by ugly truths.
At the worst,
I may never be able
to draw again.
So you see why I cannot leave this station?

Maybe I'll stay with you, and help others continue their journey through life.
My... My dear, I won't lie to you. You are right. Sometimes even the most honest mistakes can change your perceptions forever.
And do what instead? No trains go back in time.
But if it helps to soothe your fears, maybe you shouldn't look at mistakes as misfortunes, but sacrifices.
I too, like everyone else in this world, have made mistakes, but only one which I'll remember as jeopardizing my faith.
It was the challenge of my life, but it helped me over come my mistakes of the future.
Beauty isn't always made of perfections, you know? Sometimes it blemishes give it strengths.

But what if I hurt others?
And you will sometime But only its misery can teach you new ways to prevent it.
... I just want life to be beautiful. I want others to relieve their sadness by seeing art that is beautiful. I want to love unconditionally.
I think you will But you won't find people to love here.
Chooooooooooooooooo
Chooooooooooooooo
This is my last piece as myself.

If I ever meet you again, I would like to see it.
I'll place it where others can enjoy its beauty.

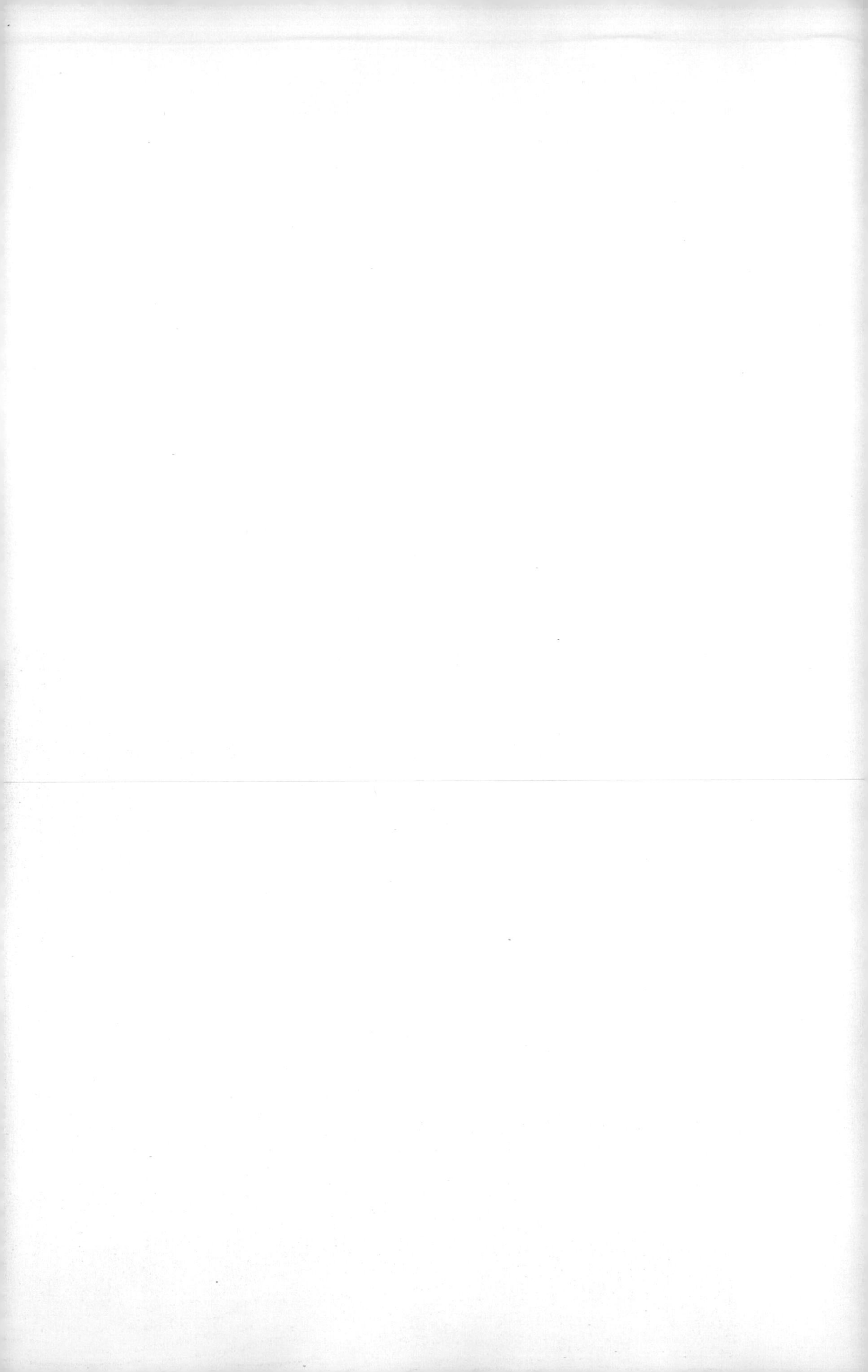

The Orange Grove

by Kazu Kibuishi

Guess who?
I thought you already left.
We're leaving tomorrow.
But there's going to be one last performance before we go.
You'll be there, right?
Of course.
Well, we have one more day, Sam...
Let's not let it go to waste.

We can perform our show to packed houses in a real theatre. Can't you imagine it? The crowds, the people.

Just promise to come with me.

I guess it doesn't matter.

Look Sam. a bird dropped a feather.

We should find one for you, too.

Here, I want you to have this.

I'll see you tomorrow, Sam.

Dad?

Can I leave work early tomorrow?

DODGSON+SON
FISHING CO.

The neighbors are leaving and they want to perform one last show.
I want to be sure I'm a part of it.

That will depend on how much work you do tomorrow.

Thank you, sir.

Why aren't you eating?

You've been quiet all week.

I need you to have your head on straight, son.
Working on that boat can get dangerous.

If you're not paying attention you could get us both killed.
POKE
POKE

Are you listening?
Or are you thinking about that girl again?

Remember, Sam.
There are plenty more in the sea.
I know, Dad.

Sam, you want some coffee?
We're gonna pull in a good load today... They're almost jumping into the damn boat...
Stop looking so sad, Sam.
It's better if you just keep your mind on the work...

It's what I did when your mother passed away...
I may have not survived if it weren't for fishing...
Oh, and you too, of course.
There's no reason to be sad...
You and I both know she isn't right for you.
You need someone stronger. A girl who can help us...
I dated an actress once. Believe me, son, when I say it isn't worth the trouble...
They're like moths flying aimlessly.
Eventually, they'll be drawn to a bright light and they'll burn up.
You don't want to be there when that happens. Trust me.
Now, remember what I told you...
Good luck, Son.

Come on, Sam!
We must hurry!

Miss Tia is in trouble!

She was swallowed up by a giant fish! Wah!

If we don't get her out soon, she will be digested!

Monkey is right. She will perish.
I am so tired.
Wah.

This way!

We have made preparations!

There is a vessel waiting for us up ahead!
It will take us to the fish!

There she is!

Shipmates, Prepare the Sail.
aye-aye

I'll find that fish if it means I search for the rest of my days...

With the courage and resolve of a hundred seafarers, our heroes set off on their quest...

We will save her, Fox.

For many months and days they battled the raging storms.

They fought ferocious Sea Horses...

and vanquished the Great Octopus...

But these battles were nothing compared to the many hardships of life at sea...

They fought starvation...

They even grew beards...

Until they finally came upon the Giant Fish...
There it is!

What do we do now, sir?

Poor Miss Tia is trapped inside the fish.
She will be digested soon. You must vanquish the beast.

No more vanquishing, Fox. I'm just going to talk to it...

There's something I've been meaning to... I mean... I...

Hey man,
You okay?
Sam,
Say your
lines.

The show's
not over.

Tia, I just...
...I mean...

So what
is it?
Do you like
her or not?
Stop it,
you guys!
Leave him
alone!

We found this little present you left for her.
It's yours, isn't it?

Stop!!

No, it's... I mean...
Spit it out!

Is it or isn't it yours?

But...
What?

Yes. It's mine.

WAHAHA HAHAHAHAHA!
HA HA HA HA HA HA HA HA

Sam and Tia sitting under a tree!
K-I-S-S-I-N-G!!
Wahaha!

HA HA HA HA HA HA HA
HA HA HA HA HA HA
HA HA HA HA HA HA HA
HA HA HA HA

I...
Sam...

I'm sorry, Tia...
Sam!

To avoid what it knew would be a most certain death, the Giant Fish conceded and lost its lunch...

Your lines are totally off.

I know.

This is the part of the story that gets really sappy.
Yeah, I know. Heh.

Heh Heh Heh Heh Heh Heh
Heh Heh Heh Heh Heh. Heh
Heh.

lap clap clap clap clap clap clap clap clap clap clap cla

lap clap clap clap clap clap clap clap clap clap clap clap

You promise me you'll be there, right Sam?

You'll meet me in the city?

Please promise me.

Sometimes I wish I could just say what I mean...

Sometimes it just isn't right...

But most times it feels as though the memory of what never was would always be sweeter than anything that could have been...

WeatherVain

by Hope Larson

She was a southern girl from a southern town.
She loved the quiet roads and the low, soft mountains, half-melted by the sun,
but far away someone waited for her.

One day she changed her clothes and brushed the sunlight out of her hair, and she rode north on a warm front blowing off the sea.

It was summer, and they were happy.
When winter came...
OW!
...it caught her by surprise.

Always cold, she became miserable.
He, however, had been cold long enough that he no longer noticed. While he was sorry for her, he didn't understand.
He gave her blankets, sweaters, the warmest coats he could find, but...

He devised a plan.
On a gray afternoon he shot an arrow into the sun....
A magnificant bird fell out of the sky and landed at his feet.

For a day and a night he worked, weaving the bird's feathers into cloth, sewing the cloth into a wonderful coat.

Tired and filled with doubt, he wrapped it around her...

...and she was warm.

She was warm, but the longer she wore the coat the more it changed her.
Her eyes became vacant, and eventually she retreated into its folds entirely.
When spring came, no matter how he begged to see her face again, she refused.

S

the end.

HEADS UP
BY BECKY CLOONAN
WITH WORDS BY VASILIS LOLOS

IT ALL COMES DOWN TO THIS
YOUR LEFT HAND OF TERMINATION
THIS IS A STAND-OFF
A TIME TO SHIVER
STAND BEFORE YOUR EXECUTIONER
A SHADOW

TAKE ONE, TAKE CAUTION
TAKE TWO, TAKE ME OUT
A CLUMSEY REACTION
I WON'T
TAKE COVER

GAT
GAT
GAT
KRSHH
TAKE ONE FOR YOU

HEADS UP I'M FALLING
HEADS UP IT HURTS
HEADS UP I'M COMING DOWN
WITH THE SWEETEST VOID IN ME

TIPS AND TOES, AIRBORN TOUCHING GROUND

TAKE A DEEP BREATH

AND FLOOD WITH YOU

TAKE MYSELF
TO FIT YOU IN
ALWAYS WAITING
LONGING FOR A PLACE TO BE
A BROKEN HEART DISEASE

tendergrass
matthew woodson

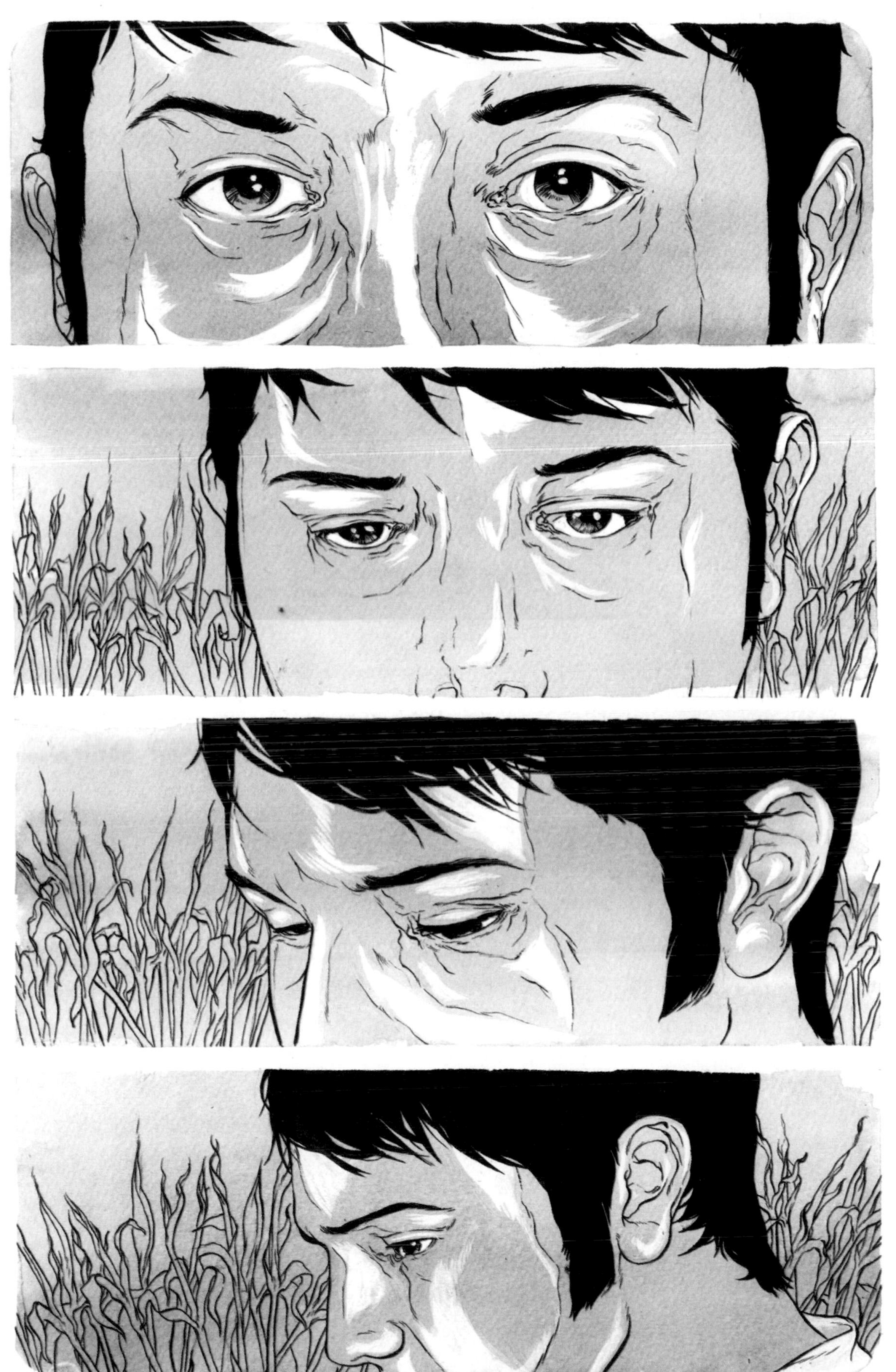

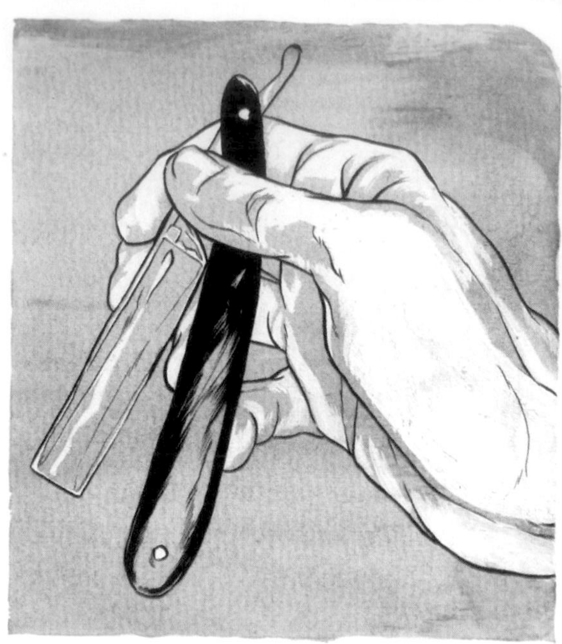
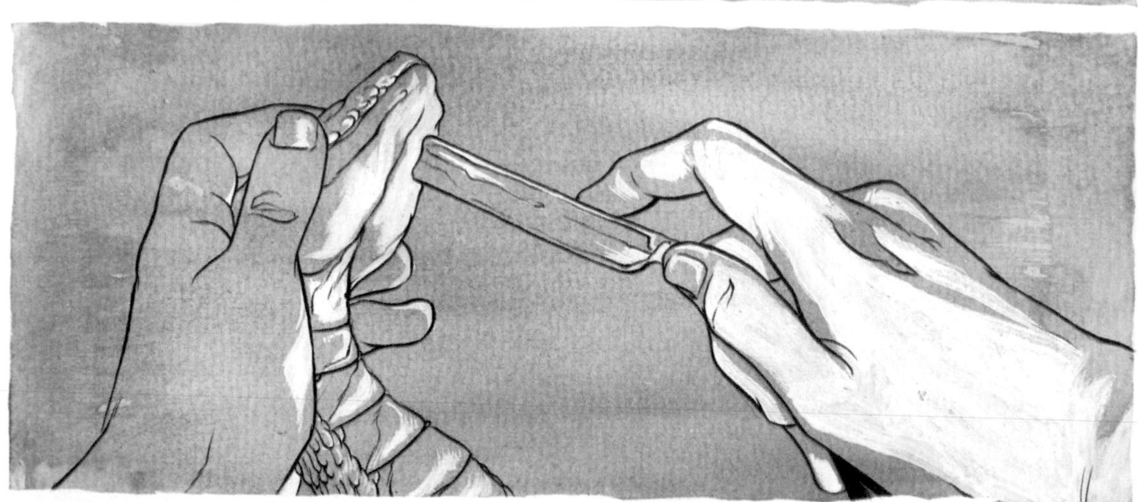

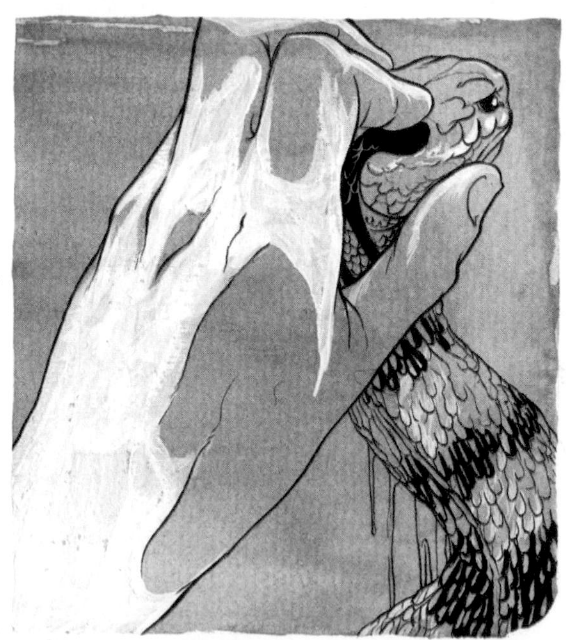

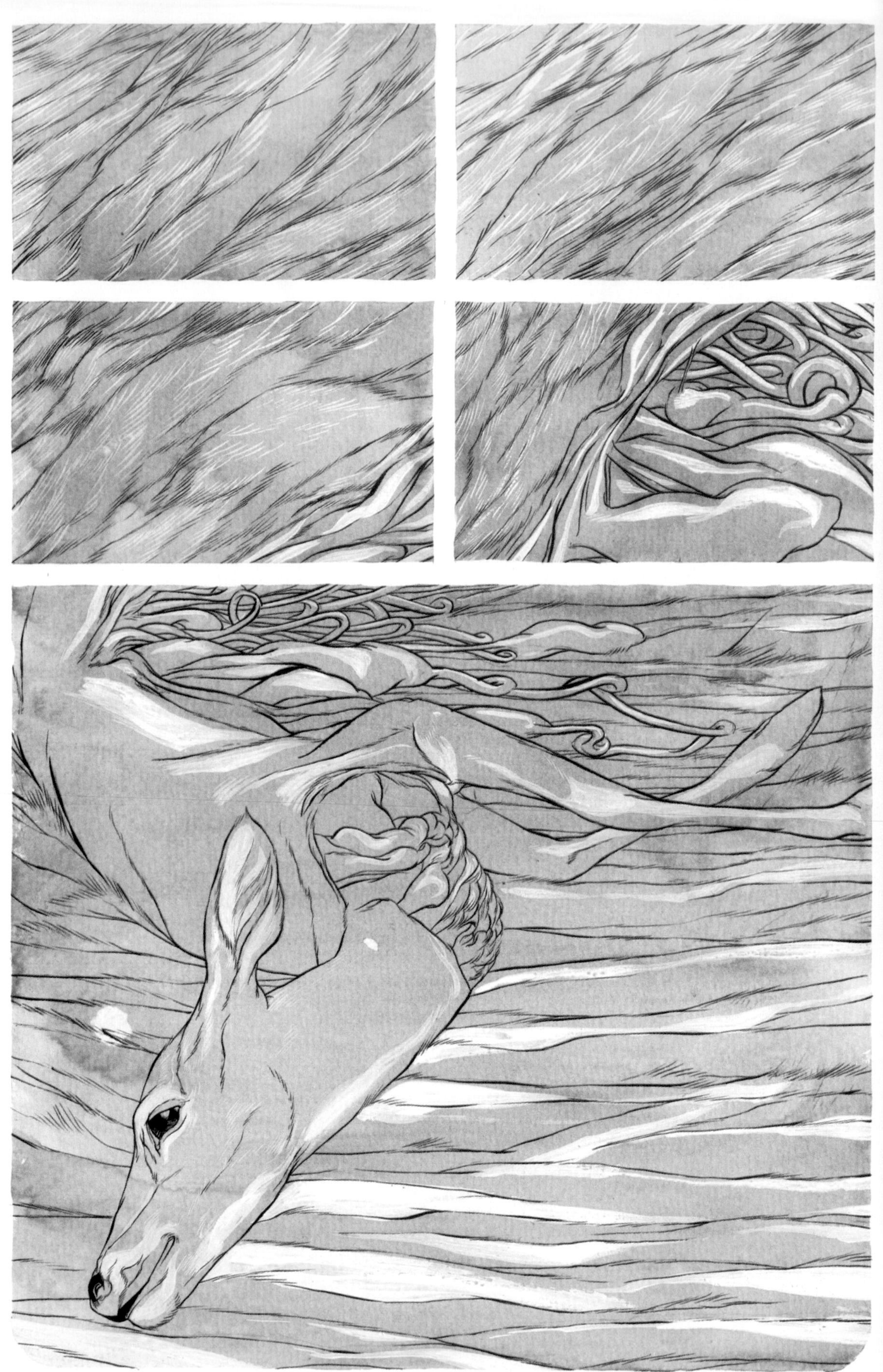

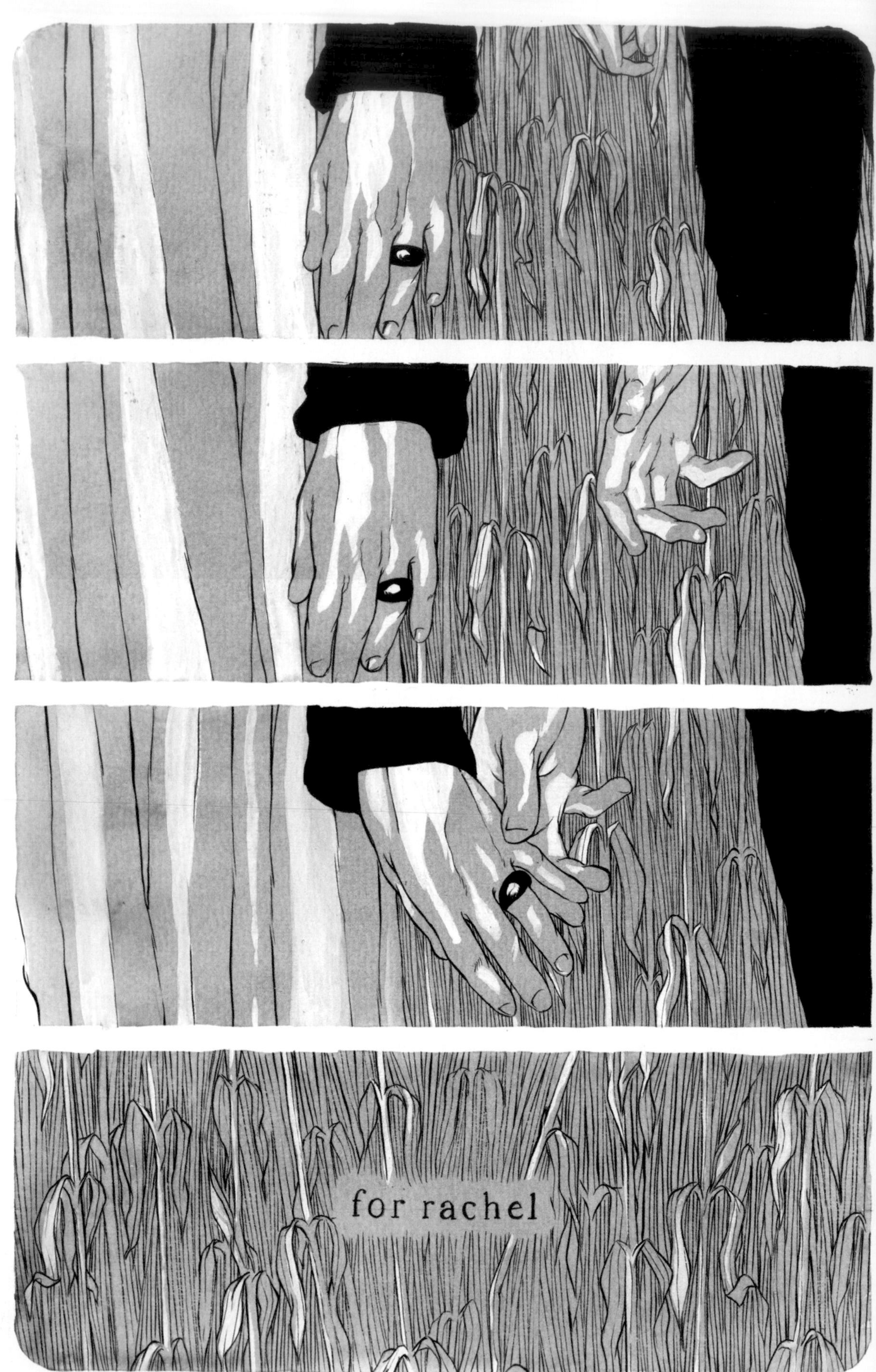
for rachel

last**things**last

by kean soo

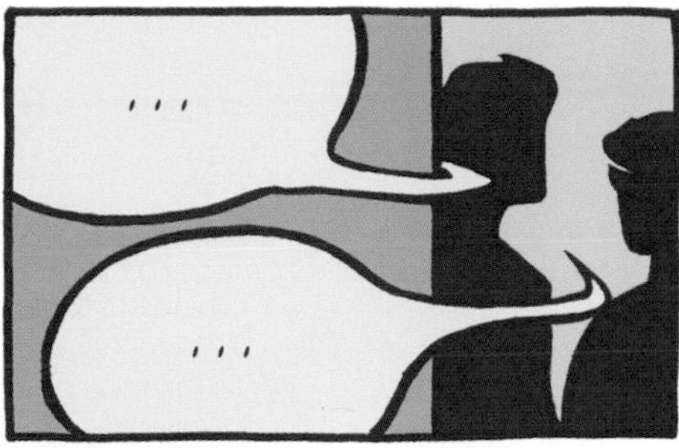

HAD TO GET
OUT OF THERE
TOO, HUH?

YEAH.

IT'S TERRIBLE IN THERE.

I DON'T EVEN KNOW WHAT I'M SUPPOSED TO SAY TO THOSE PEOPLE.

SO, UM...

HOW LONG ARE YOU GOING TO BE IN TOWN FOR?

I'M NOT SURE YET.

PROBABLY NOT LONG.

YOU KNOW, YOU LOOK OKAY WITHOUT THE HAIR.

SURE.

I SUPPOSE I SHOULD BE GETTING BACK IN THERE.

I WAS TOO LATE.

WHAT?

I CAME BACK A DAY TOO LATE. IF I HAD JUST...
...WE HADN'T TALKED MUCH IN THE PAST COUPLE OF MONTHS.

I WAS JUST SO SCARED, YOU KNOW?
I DIDN'T KNOW WHAT TO DO.

SO I DID NOTHING.

I WASN'T THERE WHEN SHE NEEDED ME MOST.

I NEVER TOLD HER HOW I REALLY FELT ABOUT HER.
AND NOW...

SHE KNEW, YOU KNOW.
SHE KNEW.

YEAH.

CELLMATES

by Phil Craven

day 12
Time seems to have slowed.
At this pace, my sentence will outgrow my ability to exist here.
If this be called existence...
Outside these walls, I know I am not forgotten (though it is no proud thing.) 
Yet I feel my own memory of life withering already.
These walls become all I know.

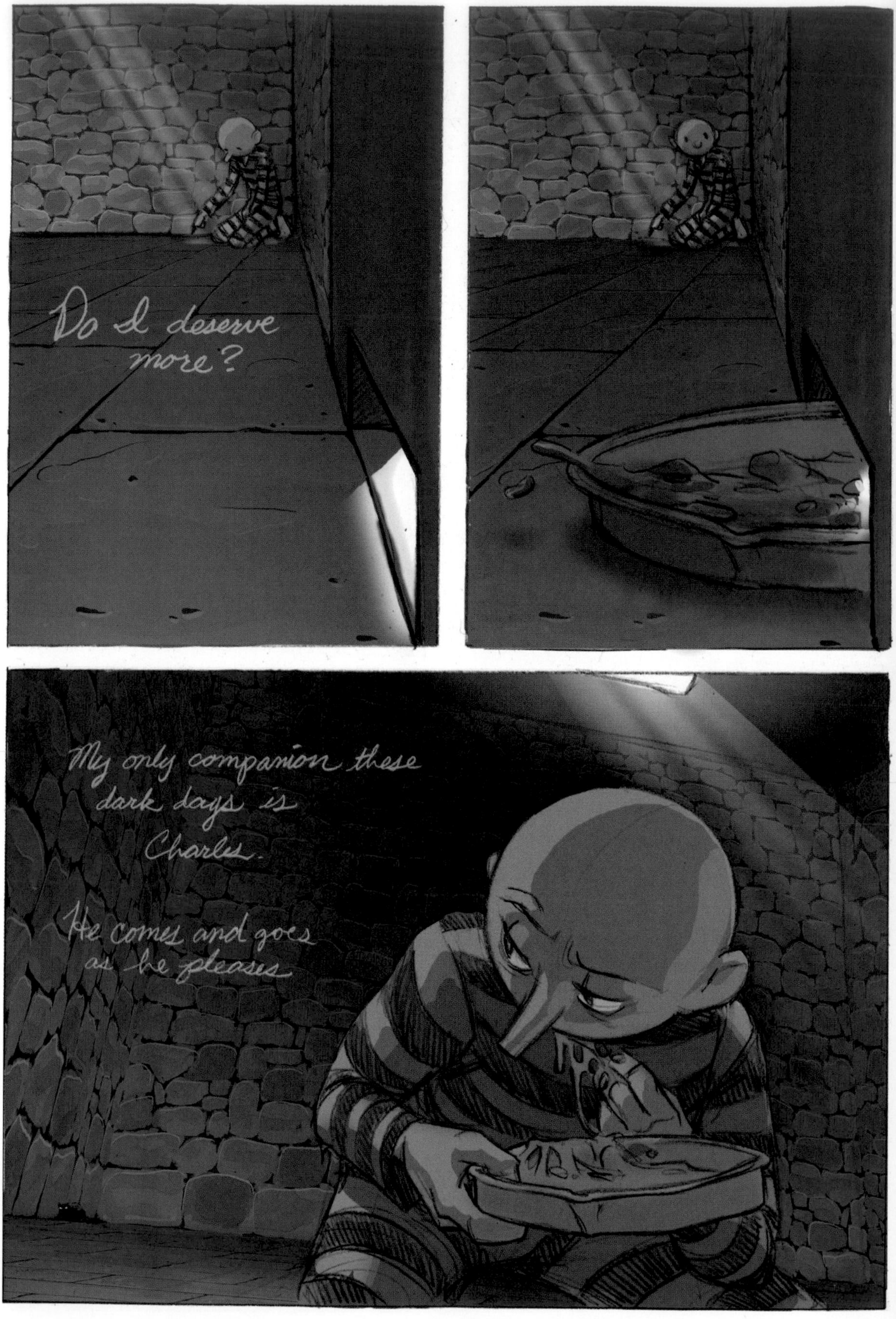

My only companion these
dark days is
Charles.

He comes and goes
as he pleases

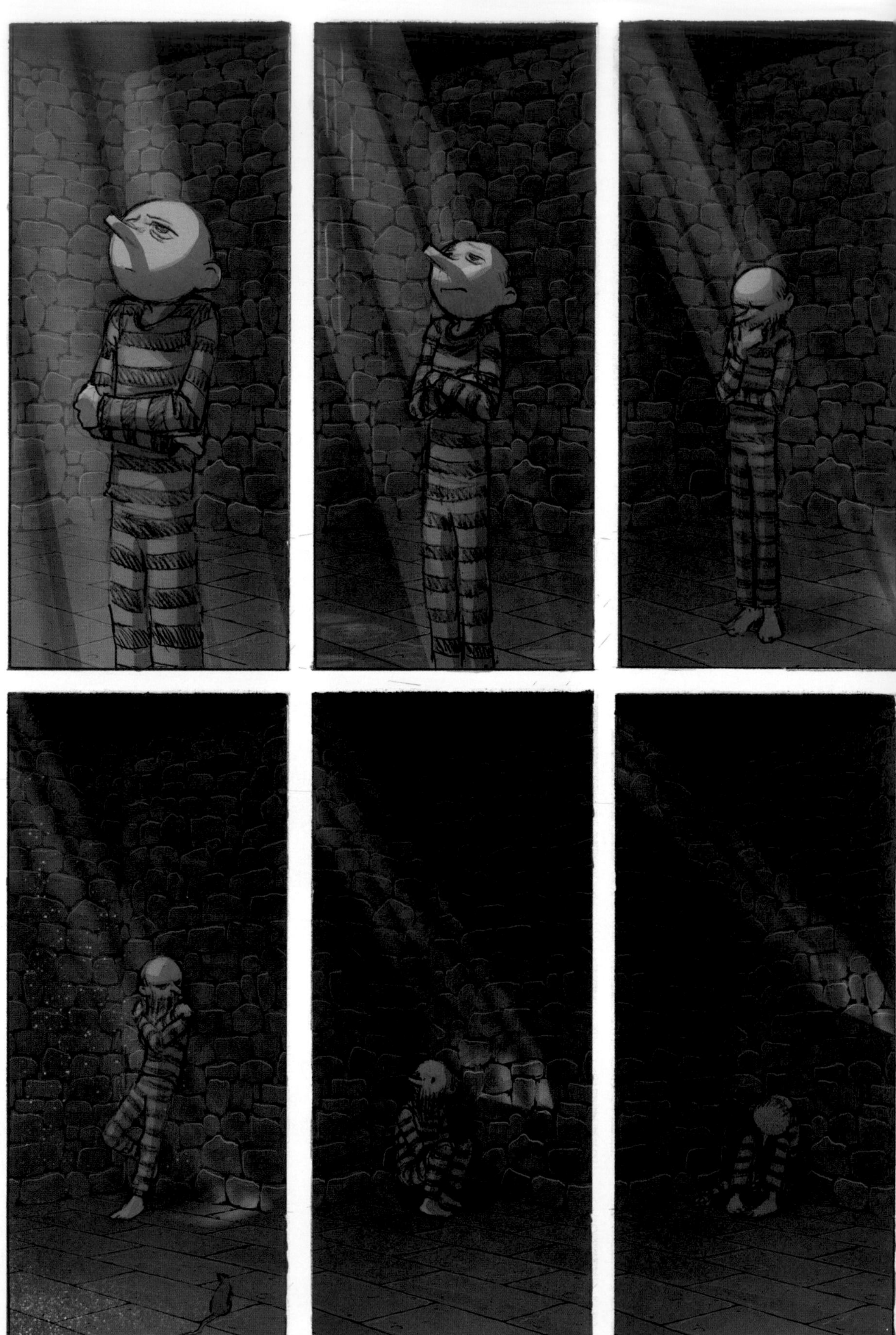

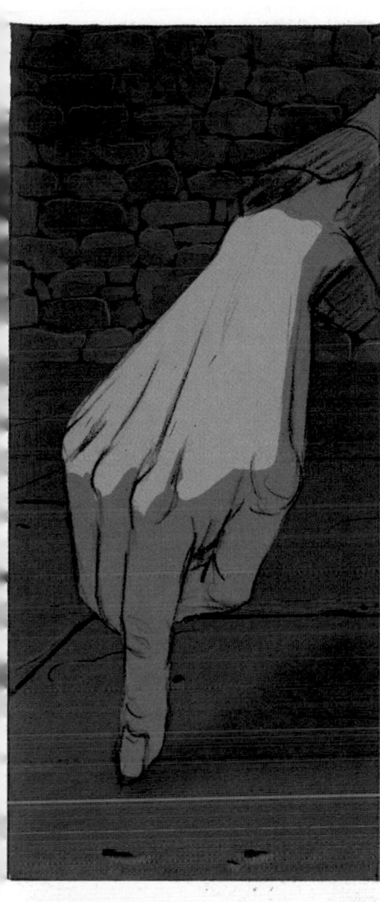

a leaf,
a twig...
bits of the
world
a world I remain in,
but not with

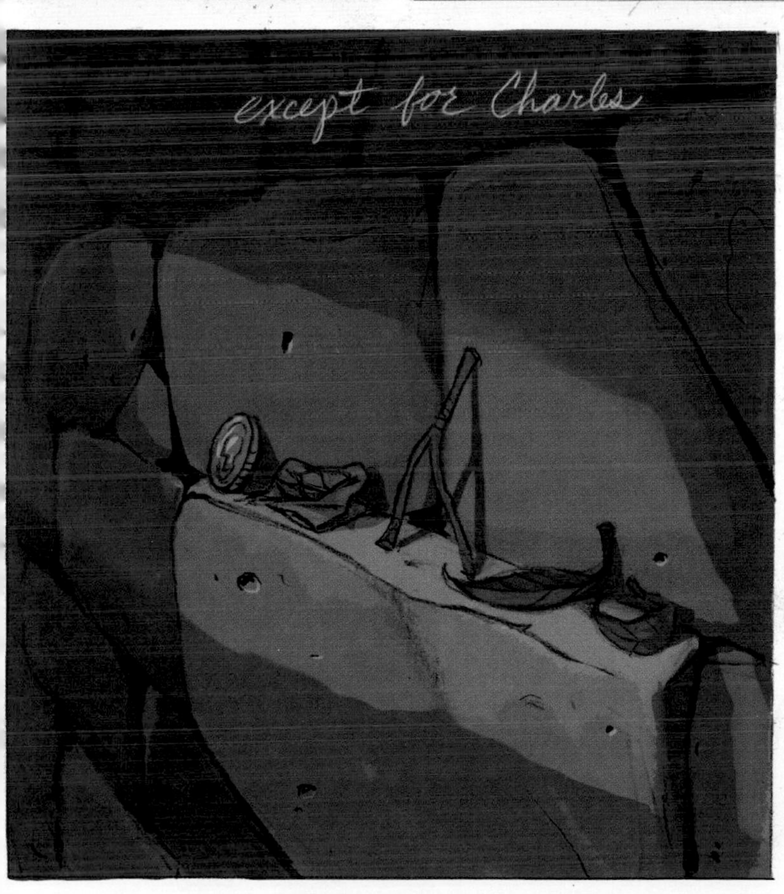

except for Charles

day —

rustlings
outside
the door
only sound

out the way I
came in?
naked,
toothless
baby with
a beard
ha ha

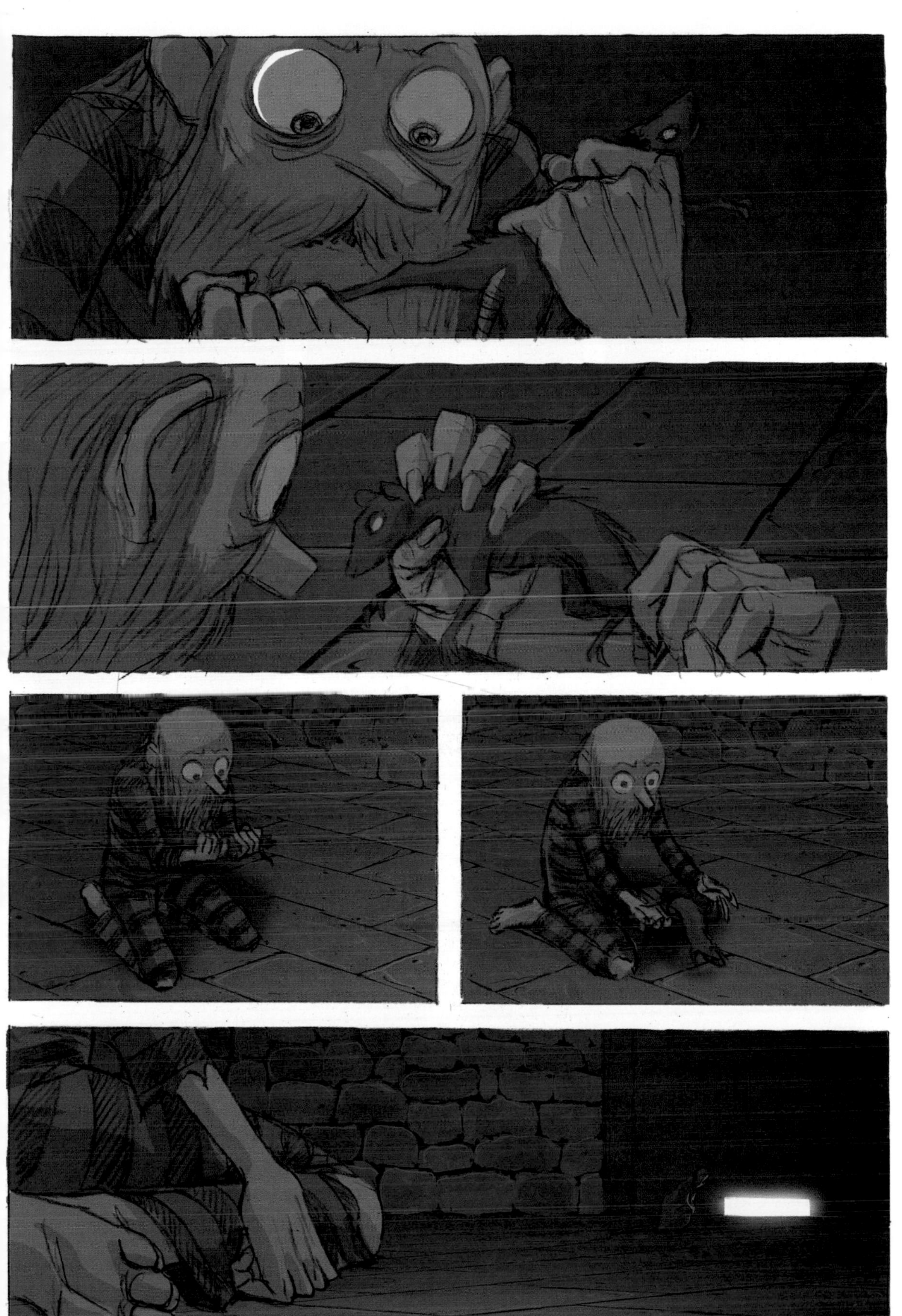

wasn't much
anyway...

The End

THE RIDE

STORY AND ART RODOLPHE GUENODEN
COLOURS KAZU KIBUISHI

ATELIERS
ALARY

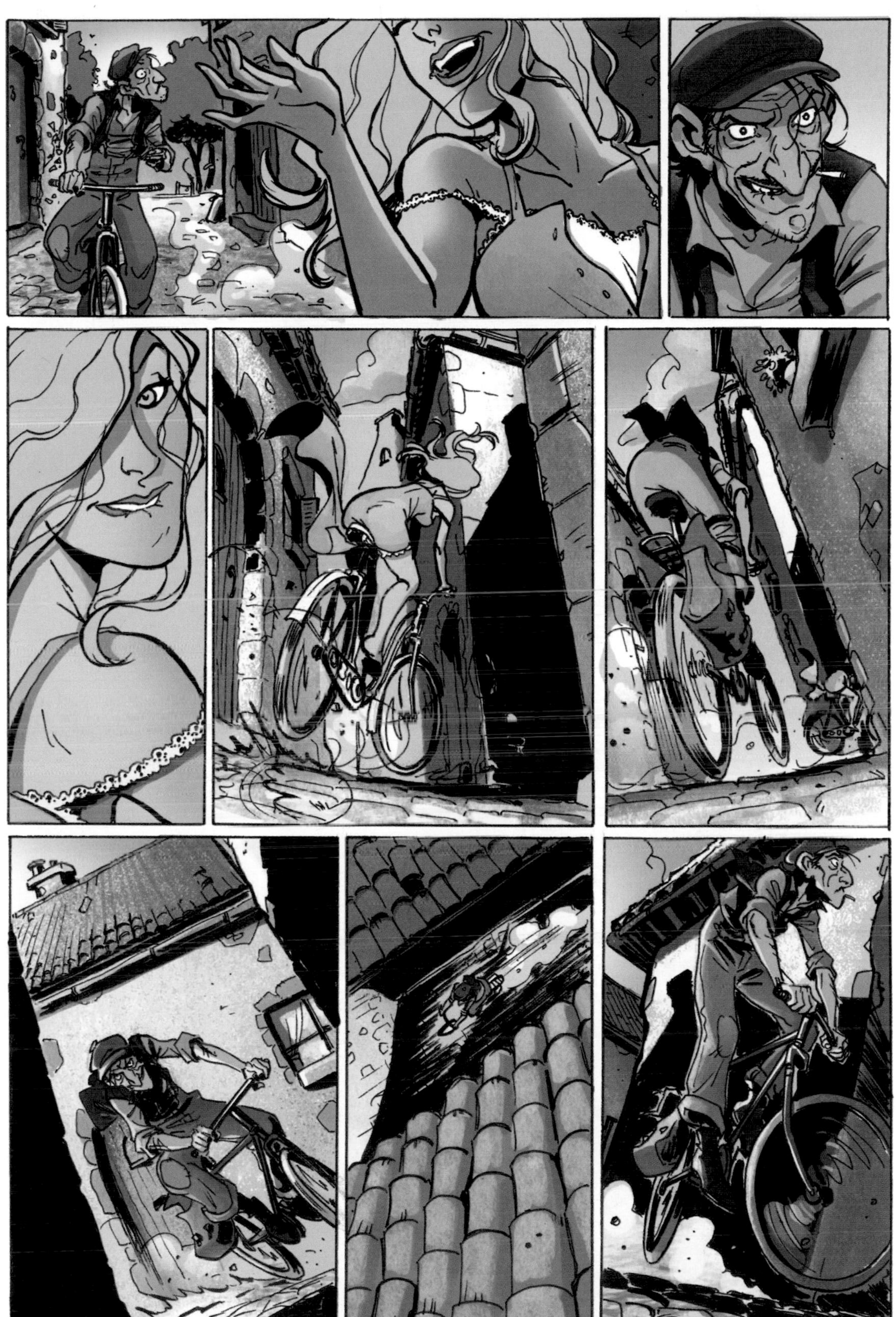

the end....

LAIKA
BY DOUG HOLGATE

PSSSH...
TINK

PLIP

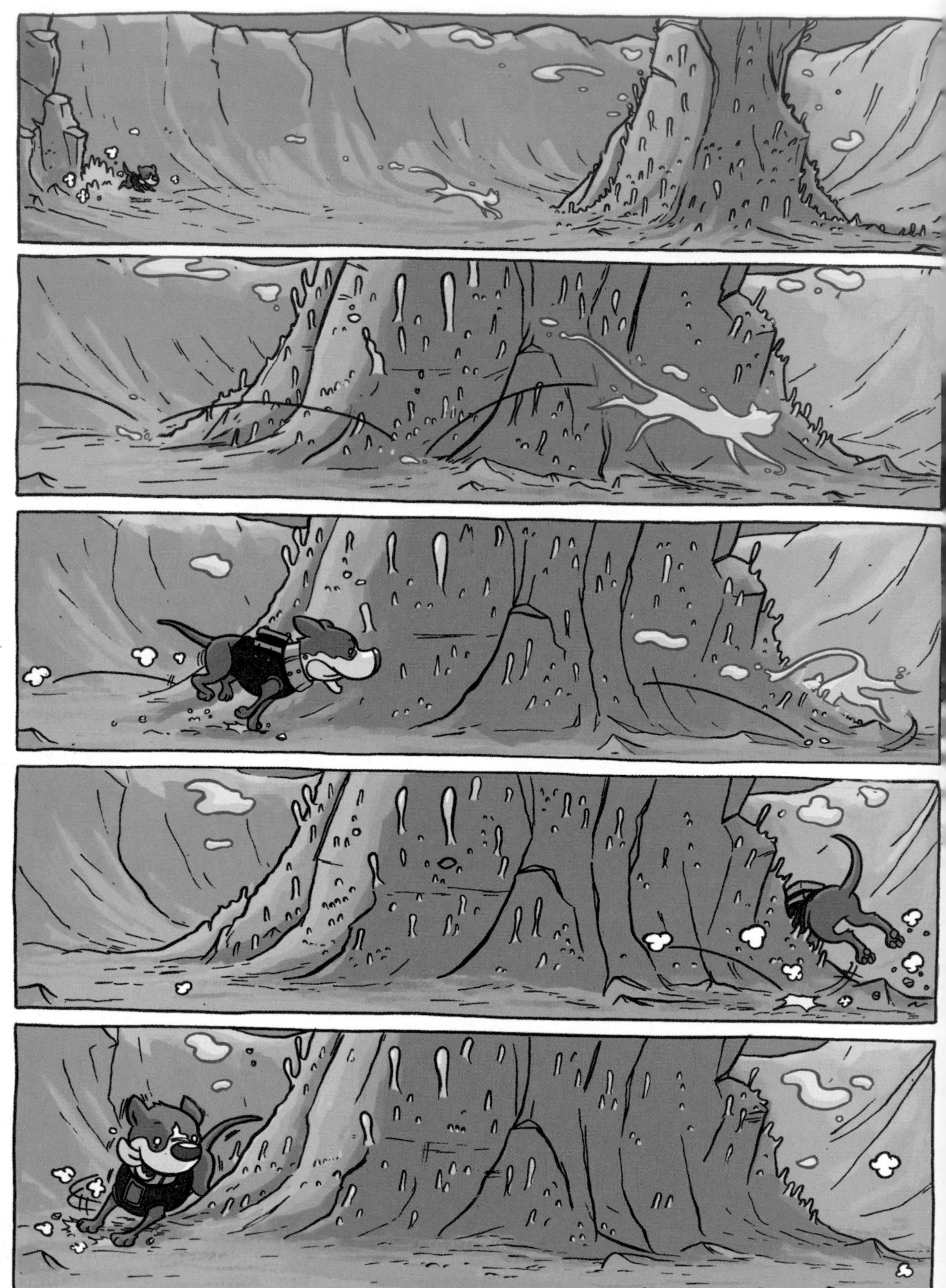

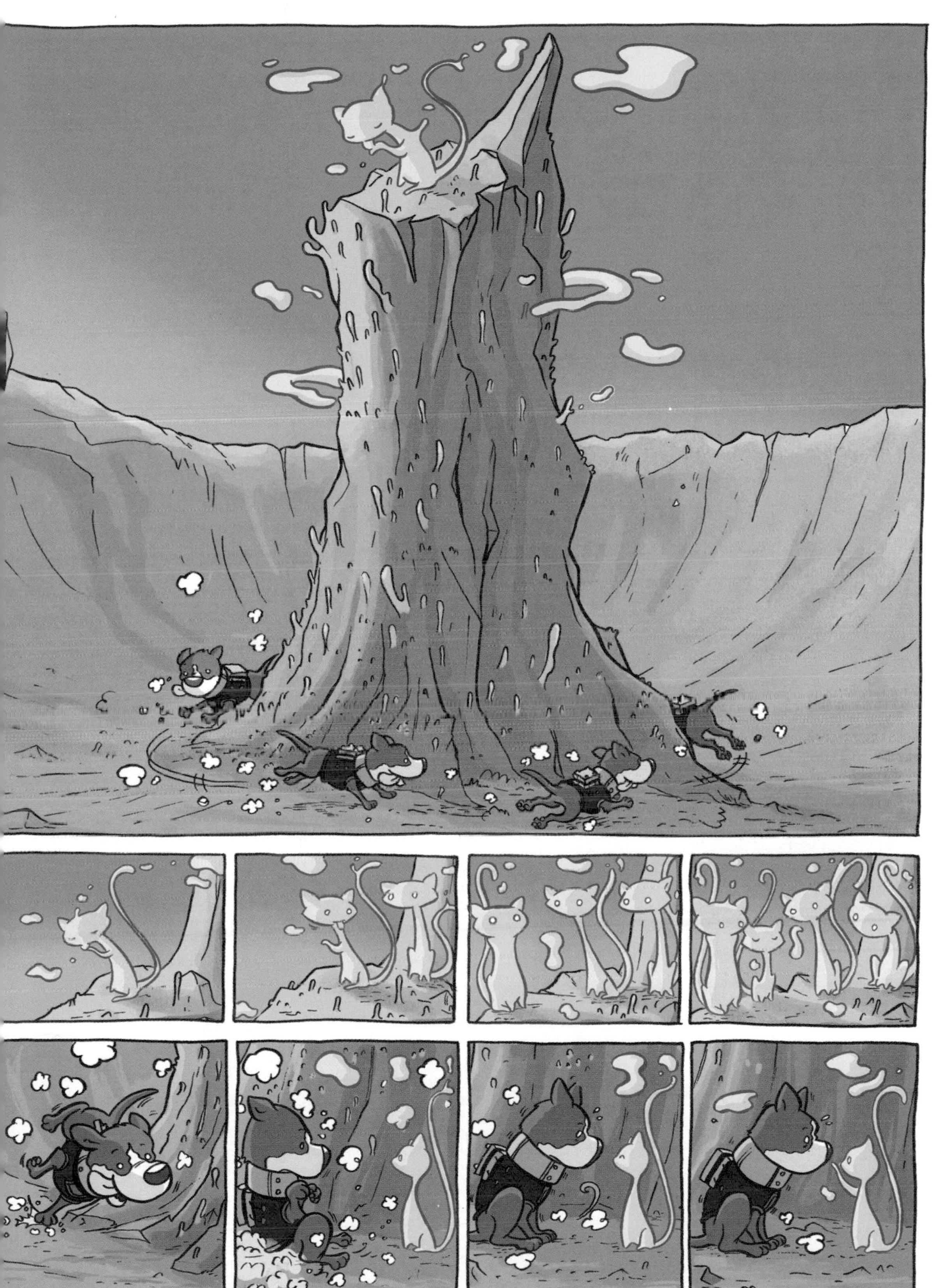

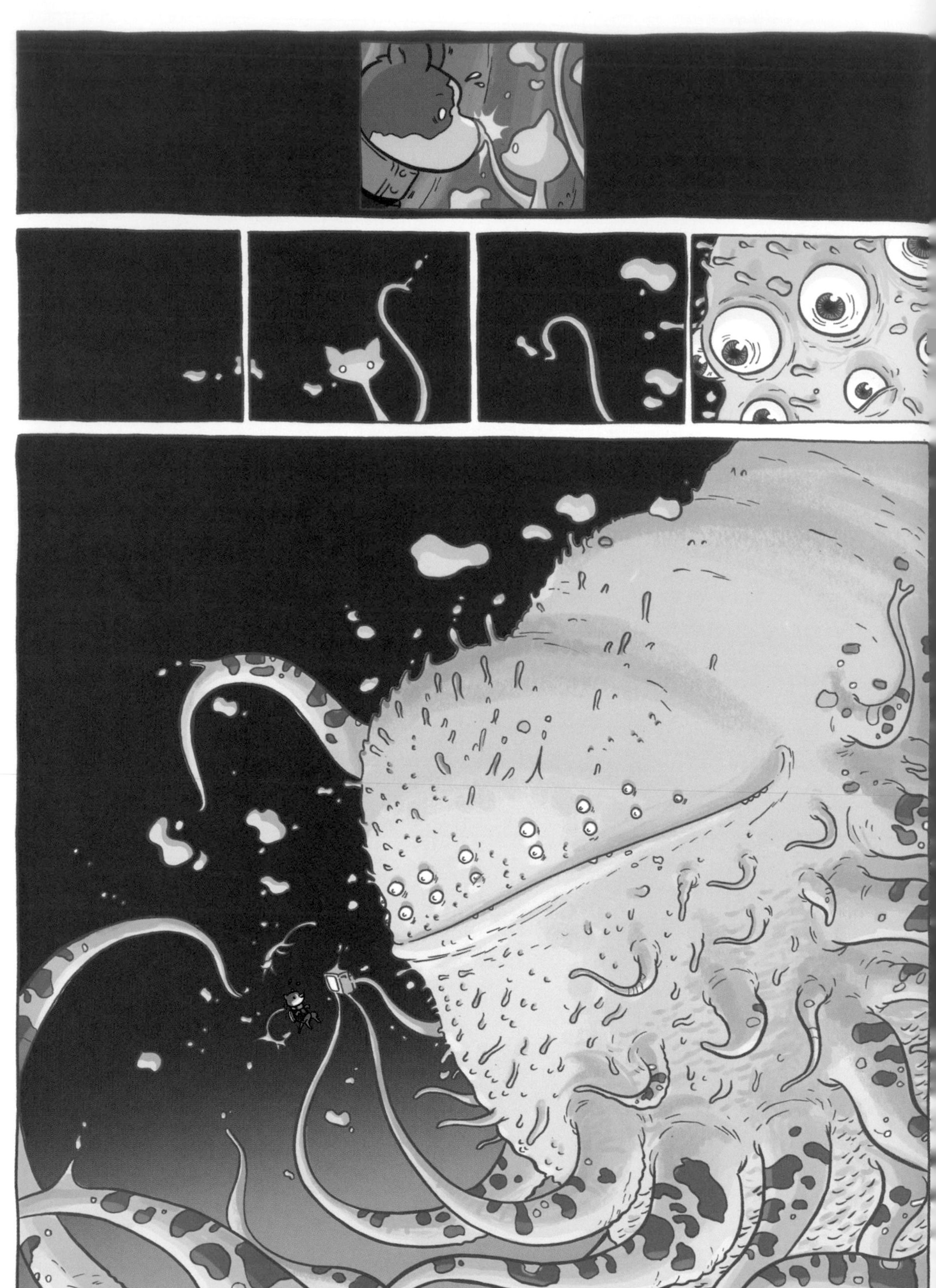

1
The Thermonuclear Menace

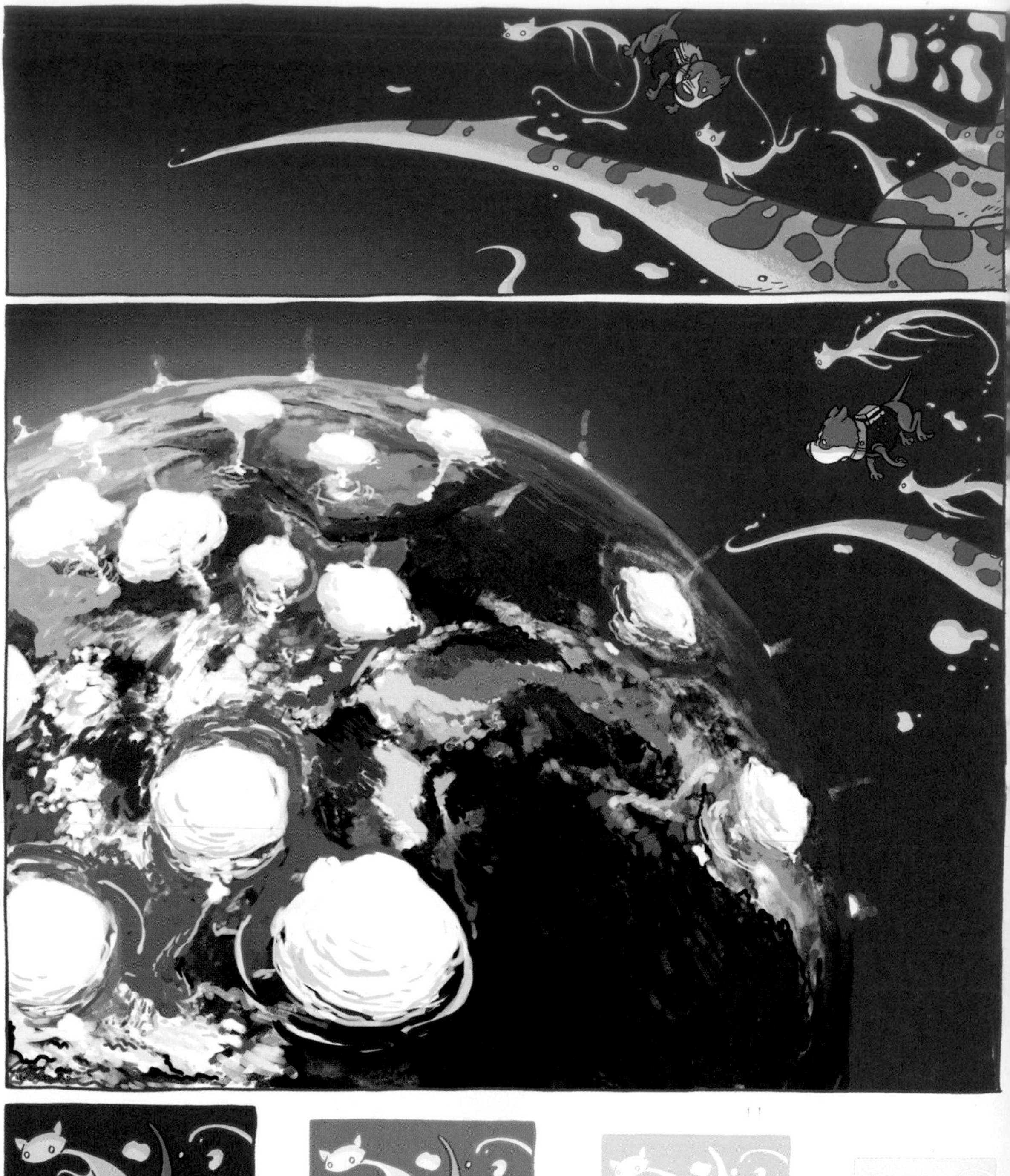

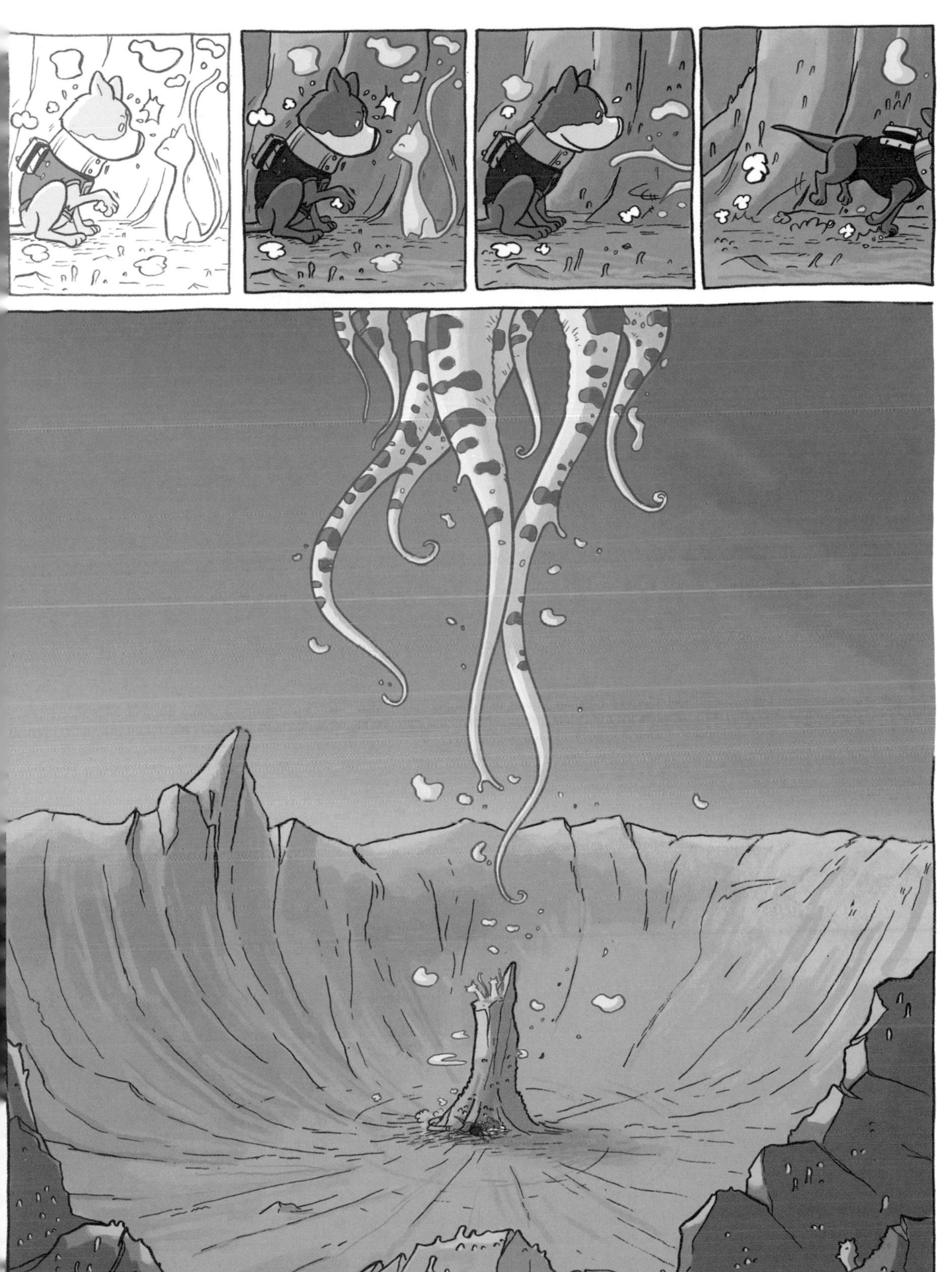

★ END ★

GHOST
TROLLEY
BY Rad Sechrist

SCRCH!

LAST STOP!
ROOTPORT

SLAM!

OFF DUTY

ARF! ARF!

HACK! COFF!

FINALLY!

I THOUGHT THEY'D NEVER LEAVE.

POOF

PURRRR!

YAWN!

SCRAPE

YOU READY BUCKET?
MROW?

MROW!
SCREECH

SSS!

HISS!

HISSS!
DEAD END
PLORP
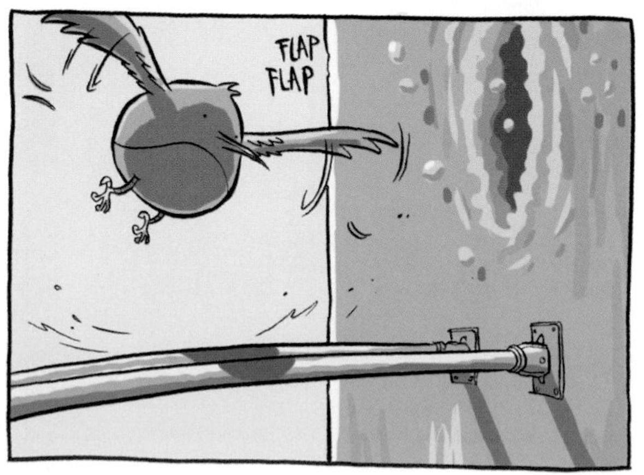
FLAP FLAP

COOO.
DEAD END

CALM DOWN! CALM DOWN! SHEESH!
HISSS!

WE'VE GONE THROUGH THAT SAME WALL LIKE FIVE TIMES.
YOU SHOULD BE USED TO IT BY NOW.

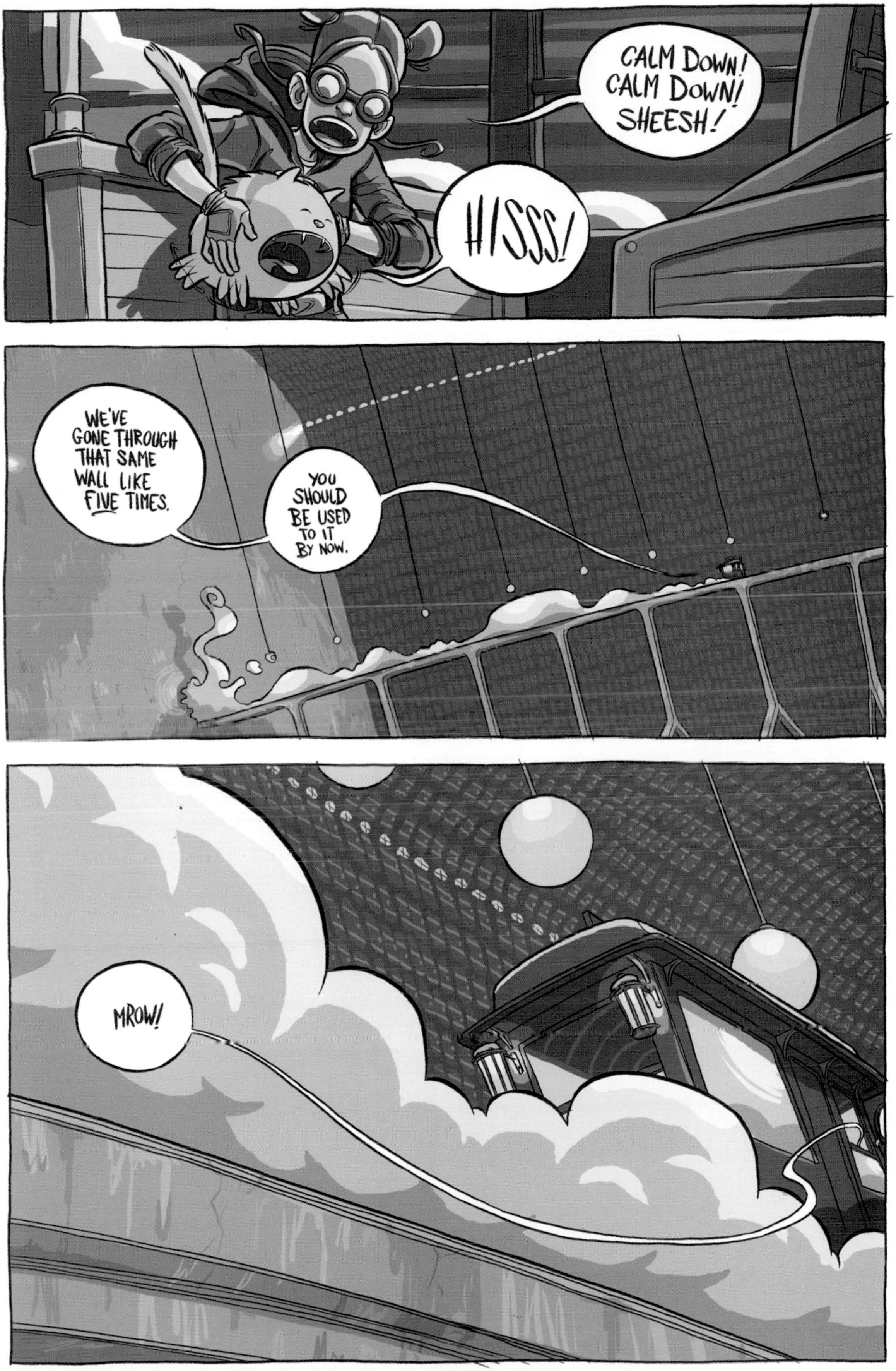

MROW!

IT'S SO BEAUTIFUL HERE, DON'T YOU THINK BUCKET?

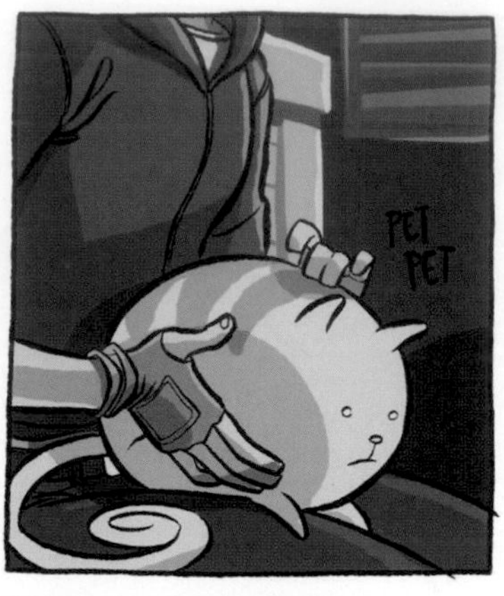
PET PET

MMEEH...

AAAAHH!
HUH?
SSSS!

AHHH!

...

AHHH!

AHHH!

WHAT ARE YOU DOING HERE BOY!?!

YOU'RE NOT SUPPOSED TO BE BACK HERE!
G-G-G

-GHOST!

BUCKET!

HURRY!
GRRR!

HISSS!
IC!
SKID

SSSS

SEE KID, NOTHIN' TO BE AFAID OF. NOW GET IN THE TROLLEY BEFORE YOU ATTRACT ANY MORE ATTENTION!

DARN KID, MESSING EVERYTHING UP.

WHAT IS THIS PLACE?
I'M NOT REALLY SURE. I FOUND IT BY ACCIDENT...
WHY WERE YOU HITCHING A RIDE ON MY TROLLEY?

DON'T YOU KNOW THAT'S AGAINST THE LAW? I SHOULD REPORT YOU TO THE AUTHORITIES!
PURRR

PURRR
UMM...
...SORRY?

PURRR
WELL APPARENTLY BUCKET LIKES YOU, SO YOU CAN'T BE ALL THAT BAD.

SO, WHAT'S WITH THE BACKPACK?
GOING ON VACATION?

NO..

.. I'M RUNNING AWAY.

CREAK

OH..
SLAM

.. I RAN AWAY ONCE.

REALLY?

YEP,

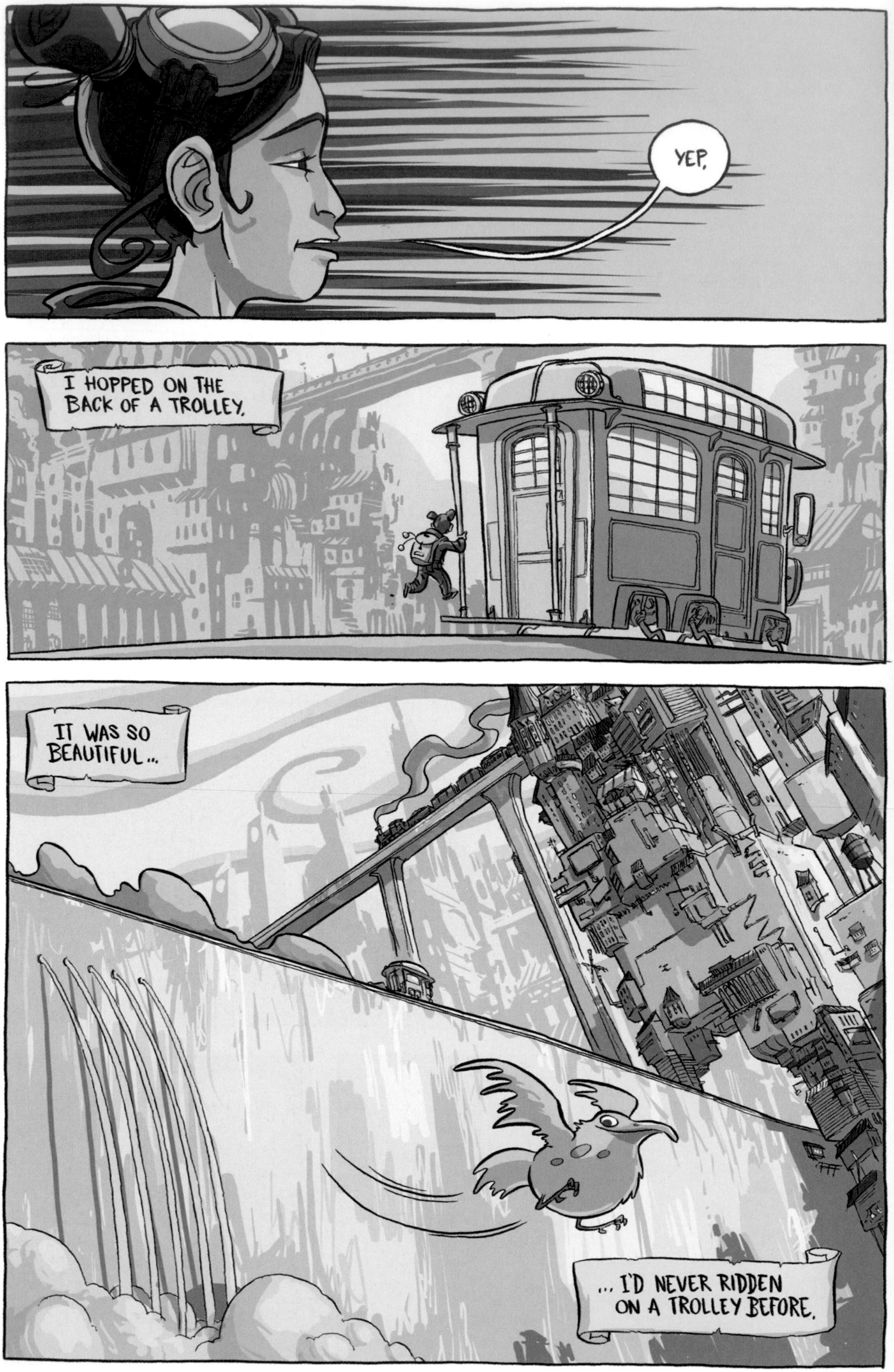

I HOPPED ON THE BACK OF A TROLLEY.

IT WAS SO BEAUTIFUL...

... I'D NEVER RIDDEN ON A TROLLEY BEFORE.

TROLLEY
THEN NIGHT CAME...
...WE PULLED INTO THE TROLLEY YARD.

I FIGURED I WOULD SLEEP IN THE YARD BY NIGHT...

...AND RIDE THE TROLLEY BY DAY.

LATER, I GOT HUNGRY. I LOOKED AROUND FOR SOME FOOD...
...ALL I FOUND WAS A BUCKET...

MROW.

...WITH A KITTEN.

I HELD THE KITTEN AS HE PURRED.
PURRR
WHERE'S YOUR MOMMY?

THEN, I STARTED TO MISS MY MOM.

THE NEXT DAY, BUCKET AND I WENT HOME.

402
MOMMY.

MROW?

SO, WHY DID YOU RUN AWAY?

YOU KNOW, I DON'T EVEN REMEMBER...
...WHAT ABOUT YOU?

MY DAD WANTED ME TO RIDE A PINK GIRLIE SCOOTER!

LOOK TOBY, I DON'T HAVE TIME TO FIX YOUR SCOOTER...
... YOU'LL JUST HAVE TO RIDE YOUR SISTER'S

YOU RAN AWAY BECAUSE YOU DIDN'T WANT TO RIDE A PINK SCOOTER?...
ISN'T THAT A LITTLE... EXTREME?

EVERYONE WOULD HAVE CALLED ME A GIRL!! THEY WOULD'VE BEAT ME UP!

YOU REALLY SHOULDN'T CARE WHAT PEOPLE THINK.

THAT'S EASY FOR YOU TO SAY, YOU'RE NOT IN THE SIXTH GRADE!
I GUESS YOU GOT ME THERE...

OH NO! I ALMOST FORGOT!..
..OUR FIRST STOP!!

WAIT, NO... YOU'RE NOT ACTUALLY THINKING OF STOPPING?!!
ARE YOU?!

JUST STAY CALM!..
.. I'M GONNA PUT SOME MAKEUP ON YOU.

OK... ... NOW TRY TO LOOK DEAD.
WHAT!?

WAIT... NO... JUST KEEP GOING!
I CAN'T, THE TROLLEY STOPS ON IT'S OWN!
BE COOL! YOU JUST HAVE TO PRETEND TO BE A GHOST.

YAWN.

SLIDE

RAH-GHAH
GHOOIG!
TAP
TAP

GHOOBI
RAAHGH?

GHOO-A-
GLUB-
PHF!
BLAH..

HEH HEH..
GLIB GHAH
GHOOO-OO-OO
AH-IC.
BLEH
IC.

BLAH
GHOO!
SHEESH!
IC
SHFP

LAST STOP!

GHA-AA--OOO!
GAAA-OOO!

THAT WAS SO COOL! I TALKED TO A DEAD GUY!!

I THINK THIS MUST BE SOME SORT OF... ...MASS TRANSIT SYSTEM FOR SPIRITS.

AS FAR AS I CAN FIGURE...
...THAT'S EXACTLY WHAT THIS PLACE IS.

ONE DAY I WAS DRIVING AND MY GEAR BROKE.
SNAP!

MY TROLLEY WENT ONTO THE WRONG TRACK.
AAHH!
HISSS!
I THOUGHT I WAS GOING TO DIE...

...THEN, POOF! RIGHT THROUGH THE WALL.
AT FIRST I ASSUMED I WAS DEAD... ...WHAT, WITH THE GHOST AND ALL...

THEN I CAME TO THE END OF THE TUNNEL...
PLORP
...AND SUDDENLY I WAS BACK.

WHEN I GOT OUT TO CHECK THE WALL...
...IT WAS WARM, BUT SOLID.

FOR WEEKS, I WONDERED IF WHAT I'D SEEN HAD BEEN REAL... ...FINALLY, ONE DAY, I JUST SLAMMED THE TROLLEY INTO THE WALL...

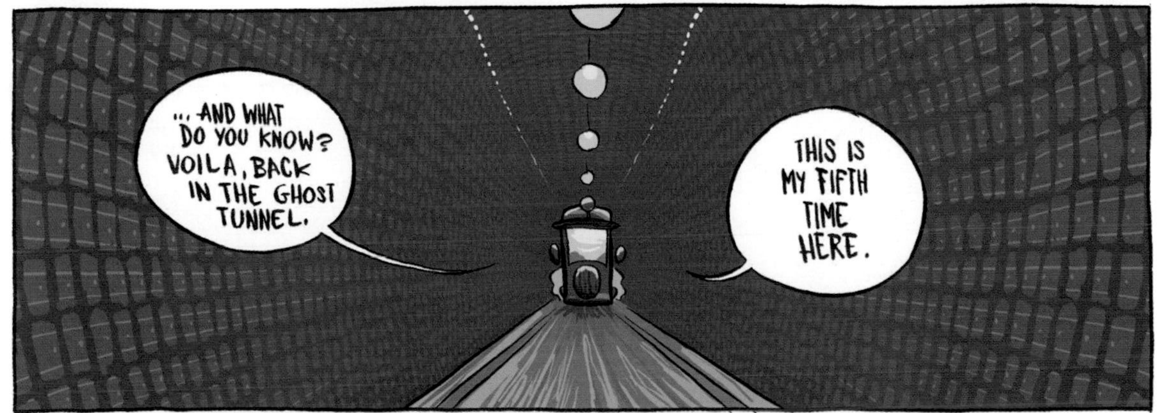
...AND WHAT DO YOU KNOW? VOILA, BACK IN THE GHOST TUNNEL.
THIS IS MY FIFTH TIME HERE.

LOOKS LIKE WE'RE COMING TO THE END OF THE LINE.

Z
Z
Z

PLORP

HERE'S MY HOUSE.

SO... ...UM... THANKS FOR THE RIDE...

...DO YOU THINK I COULD COME AGAIN SOME TIME?

SURE KID.
AFTER ALL...
...YOU STILL OWE ME FOR TODAY'S RIDE.
WINK
MROW.
The End

by Justin Ridge

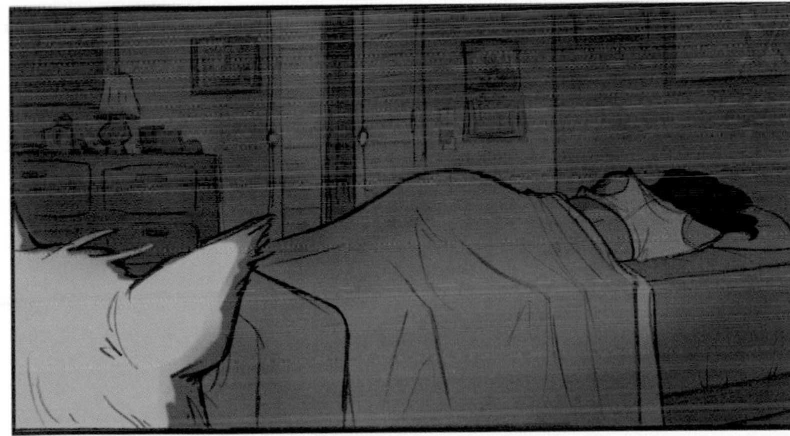

whimper....whimper

SHINK

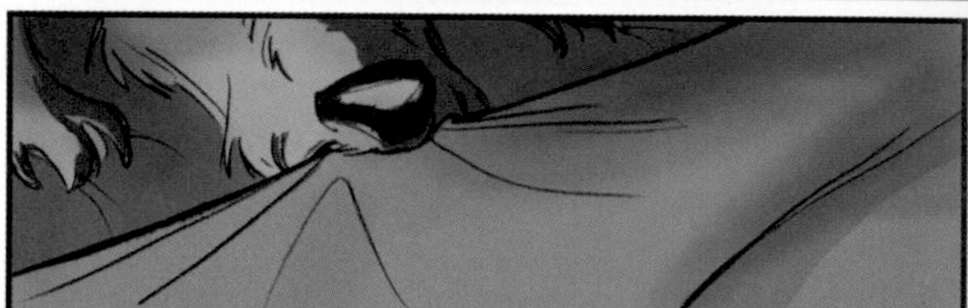

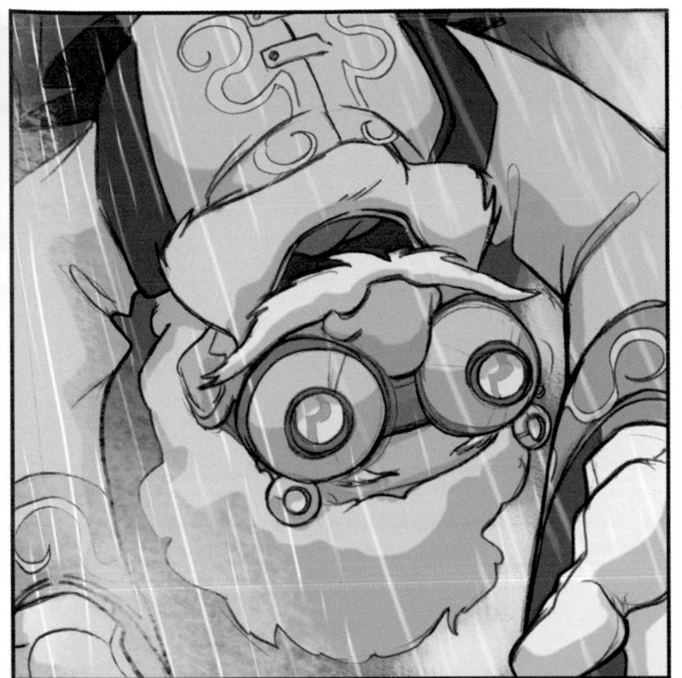
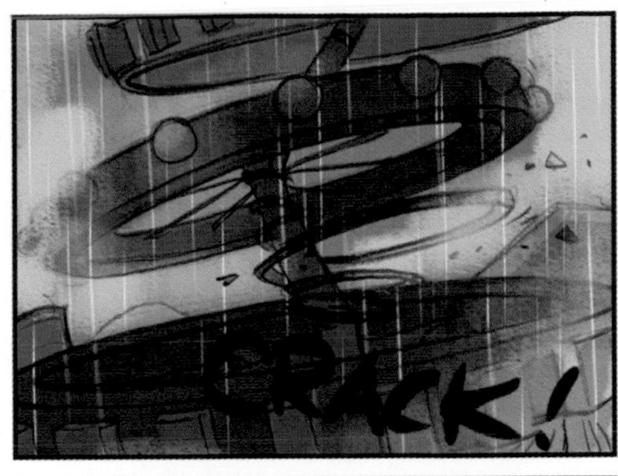
CRACK!

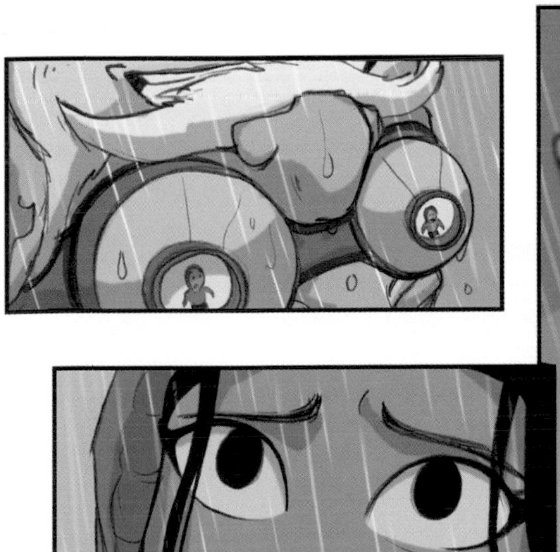

klik klik klik KLANK

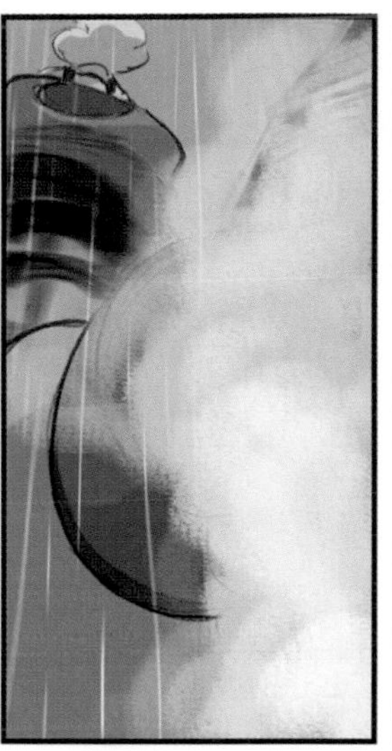

KRANK!

POOF!

POOF!

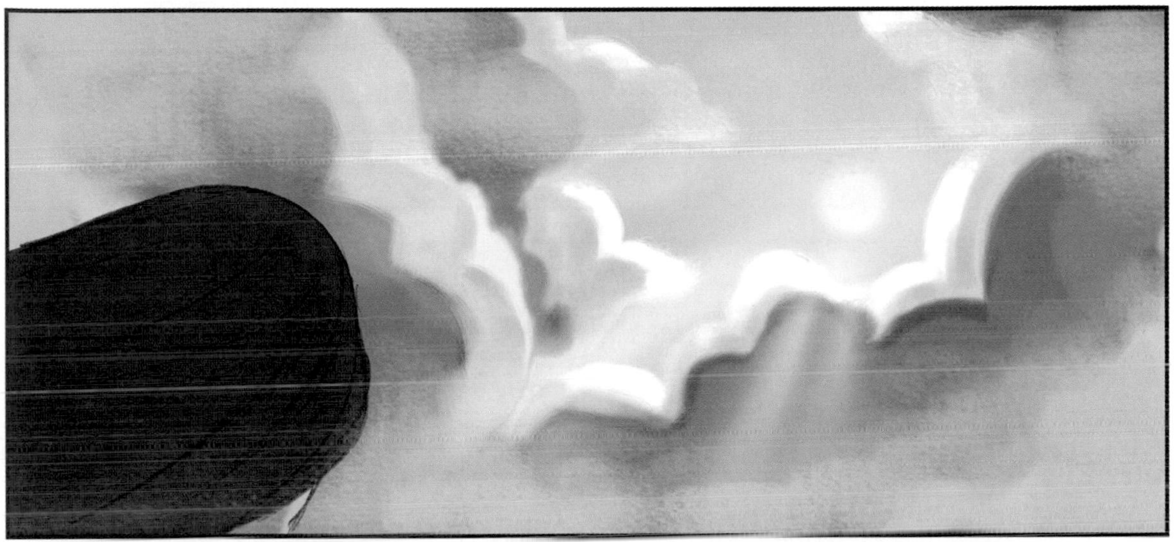

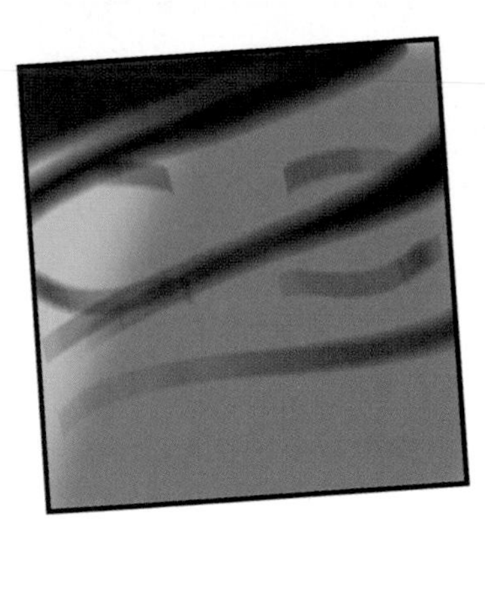

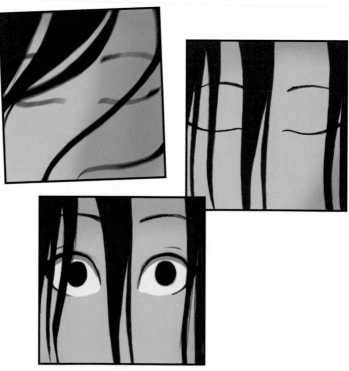

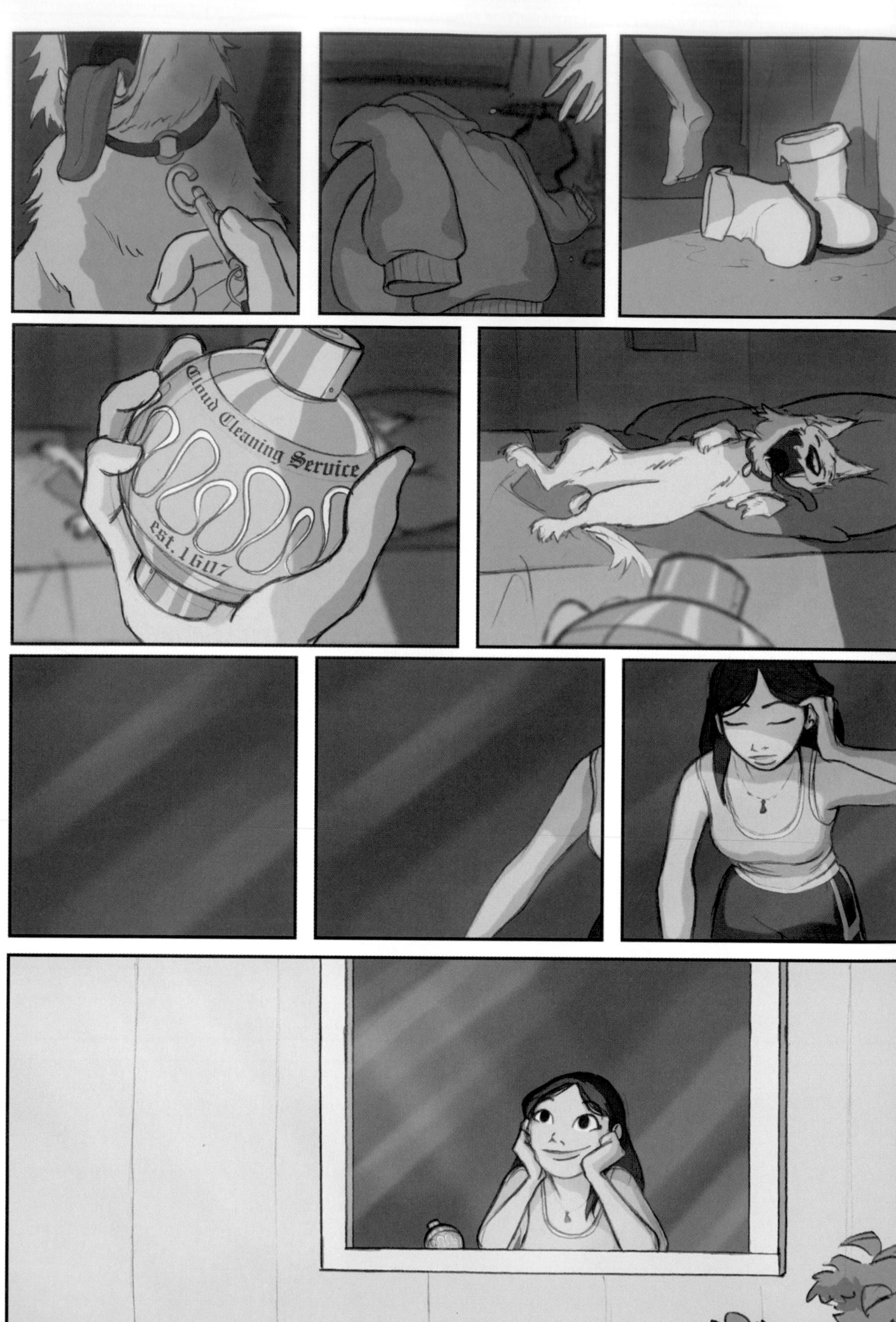
Cloud Cleaning Service
est. 1607
end.

IMPOSSIBLE
♪
SLUURP
OOPS!

SHE'S GONE!
MAJA...

AND HE'S STILL SLEEPING!
ZZZZ

HEY! WAKE UP! MAJA'S GONE
...MMUUH?

WH... WHAT?!
HURRY UP! OR WE'RE GONNA LOSE HER...

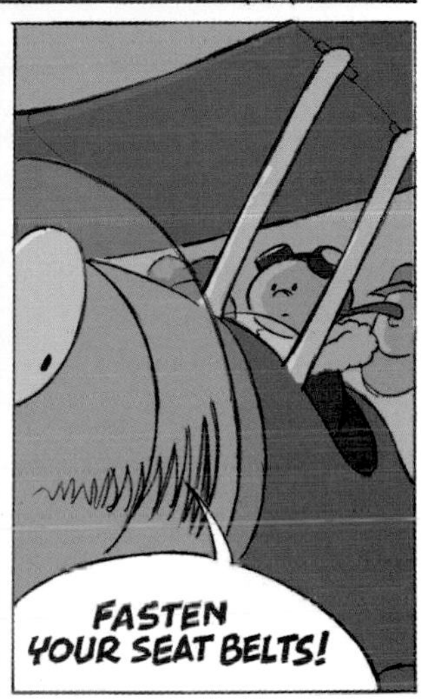
FASTEN YOUR SEAT BELTS!

VRRRRR
WHEEE!!

WATCH OUT! THE WINDOW!

VVRRRRR
WHOA!

THERE'S MAJA!

OOPS,
THIS CAN'T LAST
FOREVER, YOU
KNOW...

YEAH.
YOU'LL HAVE TO
ACCEPT IT
BUT I'M JUST
PROTECTING HER...
NO.
YOU'RE
BEING
SELFISH!

BUT I...
WE'RE GONNA
CALL YOU
"MISTER BUT"
SOON...

COME ON! IT'S ABOUT
TIME TO LET HER
MEET A GUY, IF
SHE'D LIKE TO!

BUT I...
...LOVE HER!
YES, WE KNOW!
THANKS!

IT'S AN
IMPOSSIBLE
PASSION, CAN'T
YOU SEE?

MISTER
BUT,
EH EH!

BUT I...
OOPS!
ARIS - HERVAL 2004

I M P O S S I B L E

ILLUSTRATIONS - **HERVAL** STORY - **ARIS**

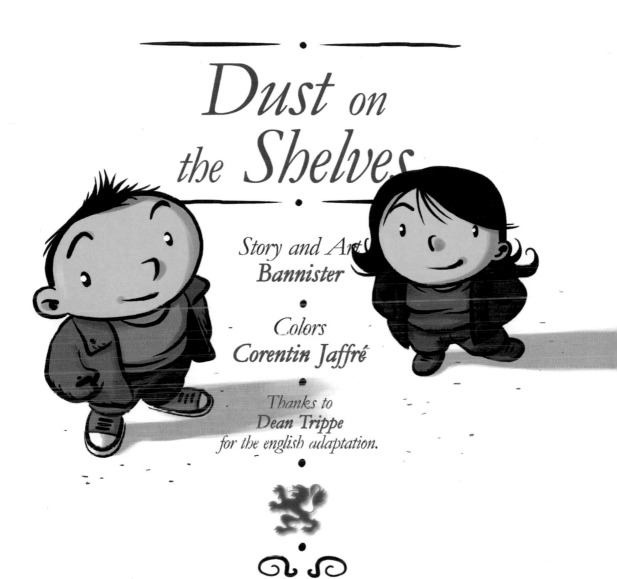

Dust on the Shelves

Story and Art
Bannister

Colors
Corentin Jaffré

Thanks to
Dean Trippe
for the english adaptation.

AFTER MY MOVE TO THE BIG CITY, I VERY QUICKLY DISCOVERED THE COMICS STORE.
COMICS-BD-NOVE

HELLO.
HI.

HI !
HELLOO !

ONLY THIS ONE FOR YOU THIS WEEK.
FINALLY. GREAT.

GOT TO GO, SEE YOU SOON !
BYE.

YOU KNOW HER ?
DOES SHE COME OFTEN ?
SHE READS MANGA TOO ?
YOU KNOW HER ?

I'M TELLING YOU! SHE'S SUPER CUTE AND SHE READS MANGA!
AH...
GREAT.

SHE READS COMICS TOO!
SHE'S LIKE...
A GIRL THAT READS COMICS!

SHE'S ARRH!!

THE OWNER SAYS SHE COMES EVERY MONDAY EVENING.
LET'S SEE THAT, THEN!

HI.
HI...

I'VE GOT NOTHING NEW FOR YOU SINCE SATURDAY, YOU KNOW...
ERR. YEAH. I KNOW...
YEAH.
HEH HEH

HI!
HELLO FLO!

IT'S HER!
THERE...

WEEKS PASSED BY
GOT MILK?

I WAS THERE
COMICS JOURNA
MAI THE PSYCHIC GIRL
EVERY MONDAY.

I'VE GOT TO TALK TO HER!
RIGHT NOW!
NOW!
...

HEY!

YES?

ERR... DID YOU JUSTCOME OUT OF THE BOOKSTORE?
BECAUSE, ERR...

'CAUSE I CAME OUT OF IT TOO...
AH
YOU LIKE MANGA?
YEAH
AND COMICS TOO?
KINDA
COOL
I DRAW TOO...

IT'S NOT EASY TO TALK TO A GIRL FOR THE FIRST TIME...
ShoeS
ESPECIALLY IF YOU'RE A BOY.

AFTER THAT, WE BECAME FRIENDS.
YEE-HAAA !!
IN THEATER NEAR YOU

WHERE ?
HERE, HERE !
SHOUJO MANGA ! FINALLY !
HEH HEH
PREVIEWS

AND ONE DAY, MONTHS AFTER OUR FIRST MEETING...
SEE YOU THURSDAY ?
YEAH

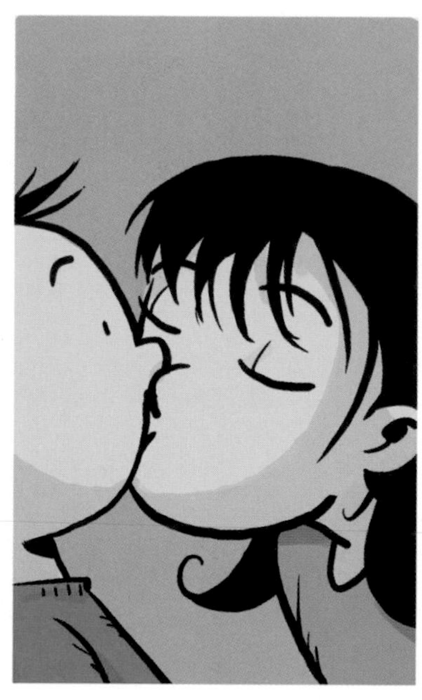

BEEEEEE

WE DON'T GET OVER TO THE BOOKSHOP MUCH NOW, BECAUSE WE LIVE TOO FAR.

BUT EVERYTIME I OPEN THE DOOR -THAT DOESN'T CLOSE WELL- EVERYTHING COMES RIGHT BACK.
ATARI

THE OLD FRIENDS ARE STILL THERE. THE DUST ON THE SHELVES TOO.
NOTHING'S CHANGED.

AT LEAST, I'M HOPING THESE LITTLE THINGS WON'T.

SOME CHANGES ARE INEVITABLE THOUGH...

IT WAS FIFTEEN YEARS AGO, THE FIRST TIME I STEPPED INTO THIS BOOKSHOP. IT WILL ALWAYS BE THE PLACE MY LIFE CHANGED FOREVER.
COMICS-BD
THE END?

by clio chiang
2005

HUFF! HUFF!
HEY!
HEY, STOP!
CARDBO
ONL

PACIFIC CENTRE MALL
750
MALL

~SNIIIIIIFF!
?!
PICK!
PICK!
PICK!
PICK!
PICK!
HEY!!
THOSE ARE PRIVATE PROPERTY!
!!

STOP!!
STAR FRUIT
100% JUICE
?
?
I'VE...
GOT..
YAAIGH..!!
AW!!..
....

TAK!
TAK!
TAK!
TAK!
TAK!
!!
PPWHSS

PFFFT...
CHICKEN.

BLIP POP

by RYAN SIAS

EXCUSE ME MADAM, BORED WITH EVERYDAY LIFE?
BLIP POP IS AN EXCITING NEW DRINK THAT CAN CHANGE YOUR LIFE!
YEAH.
OH PLEASE.
IT'S TRUE! GET OUT OF THIS DREARY LIGHT AND GO UP ABOVE THE CLOUDS INTO PURE SUNLIGHT!
BLIP'S PATENTED FLYING BUBBLES WILL LIFT YOU UP UP AND AWAY!

GLUB
GLUB
GLUB
GLUB
GLU

YUM!
GRAPY!

WHAT HAPPENS NOW?

THIS SUCKS
NOTHING'S HAPPENING.

OH!

THESE CLOUDS ARE SOFT.

I'M NOT GOING TO LET YOU EAT MY CUTE NEW FLYING FRIENDS!

HIYAH!
SQUISH!

WAAHHHH

WAAHHHHHH

URPP!

MY BUBBLES!

AWH CRAP!

AHHH

HHHHH
AAAAHH

BUBBLES?

WHAT JUST HAPPENED?

YOU HAD SO MUCH FUN WITH ME THAT YOU DIDN'T WANT TO SEE ME DIE?

THANKS!

BYE, BYE BUBBLES.
IS SHE TALKING TO BUBBLES?
YES, THIS STREET IS GETTING REALLY WEIRD.

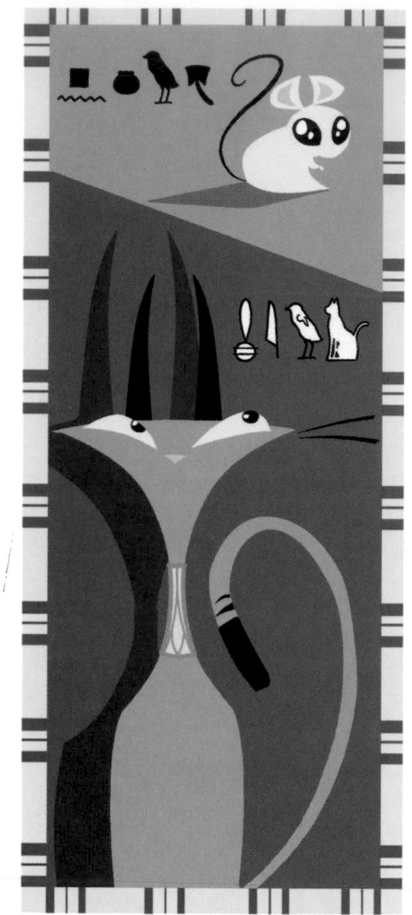

▲ MOUSETRAP ▲

STORY AND ART
JOHANE MATTE

COLOR
GHISLAIN BARBE

SPECIAL THANKS TO
ERIC BAPTIZAT

WHOMP!
WHOMP!
WHOMP!

SPLITCH!
GROWL
FROWL!
MROWL!
SCROWL!

Z

SPLOUSH!

THE WILL OF THE GODS IS READ IN THE STARS BUT WE MUST ALSO WATCH FOR ANY UNUSUAL SIGN.
SPLISH
SPLASH

SPLISH SPLASH

WET CAT?
"PROJECT FAILURE"
REALLY? I WOULD HAVE SAID "BAD FLOOD".
YOU STILL HAVE MUCH TO LEARN.
SPLISH SPLASH

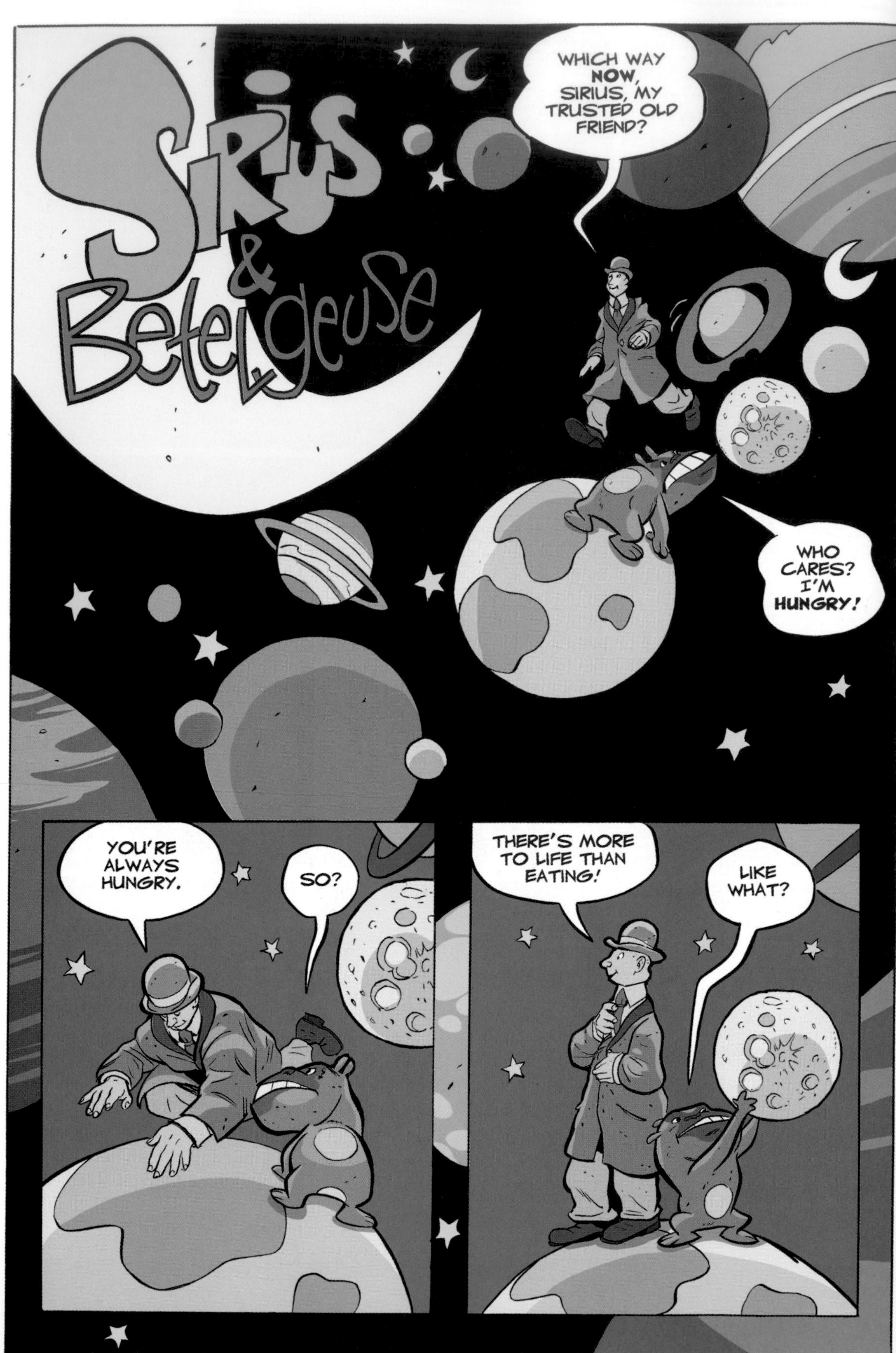
Sirius & Betelgeuse
WHICH WAY NOW, SIRIUS, MY TRUSTED OLD FRIEND?
WHO CARES? I'M HUNGRY!
YOU'RE ALWAYS HUNGRY.
SO?
THERE'S MORE TO LIFE THAN EATING!
LIKE WHAT?

LIKE WALKING ACROSS THE UNIVERSE!

THERE'RE ALWAYS NEW PLANETS AND STARS TO EXPLORE!
BORING! THAT'S WHAT WE DO EVERY DAY!

WHY DON'T YOU ENJOY IT, INSTEAD OF GOBBLING EVERYTHING UP LIKE IT'S GOING TO VANISH TOMORROW?
I'M JUST AS GOD MADE ME . . .

AND IF GOD MADE ME HUNGRY, THEN BEING HUNGRY MUST BE A GOOD THING.

JUST SLOW DOWN, THAT'S ALL.
SCREW YOU! I'M HUNGRY!

HE NEVER DID LISTEN TO ME.

J. SMITH

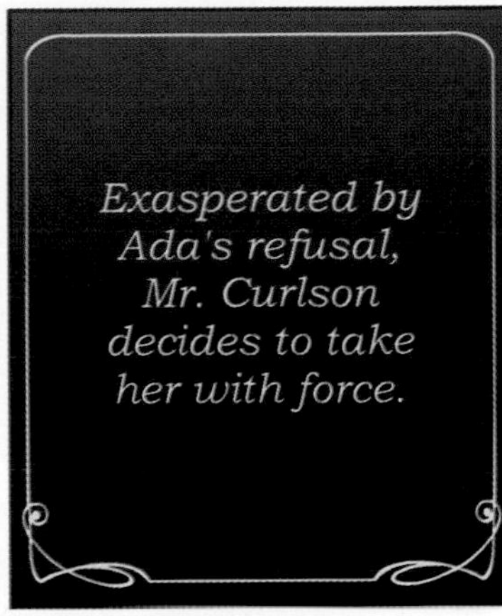

Exasperated by Ada's refusal, Mr. Curlson decides to take her with force.

THE FLYING BRIDE

Our heroes arrive...

Brake!
Brake!

The unexpected noise alarms Mr. Curlson and instills hope in Ada's heart...

Imprisoned Ada, Mr Curlson is preparing to receive the rescuers...

Is all well that ends well ?

The End

THE PLANK

BY BEN HATKE

YOU HAVE BEEN SENTENCED BY THIS CREW TO THE WATERY DEPTHS!

HAVE YOU ANY FINAL WORDS?

LOOK AT YOU. YER NO PIRATES. AND YOU'VE SEEN YER LAST SUNRISE.

WE THE CREW HAVE JUDGED YOU TO BE UNFIT FOR THE COMMAND OF THIS VESSEL. FOR A CAPTAIN SHOULD NOT MERELY BE THE MEANEST, TOUGHEST AND MOST FEARED MEMBER OF THE CREW...

THIS IS YOU!

BUT SHOULD EXEMPLIFY LEADERSHIP SKILLS, DIPLOMACY AND, ABOVE ALL, A GENTLE HAND. WE HAVE ASKED POLITELY FOR YOU TO STEP DOWN AS CAPTAIN –

S-RIGHT! AN INSTEAD OF ANSWERIN' SHE BIT ME ARM UP!

S'ALRIGHT, DEVIN. S'ALRIGHT.

RELEASE THE PLANK BOYS.
I CAN'T! IT'S STUCK! SOME ONE'S WELDED THE PINS!
TWEEEEEEEEE
AH! WHAT'S THAT? WHAT'S SHE DOING?
HEH HEEH HEEEEH!
THAT'S A CALL, THAT BE! AN ANCIENT CALL!
A CALL FOR WHAT, CRAZY TED?
LOOK SIR!
RAZOR FISH!

aaaaH!
THUNK
YaR HaR HaRR!
SLICE!
SIR! NaTTIE'S LOOSE!
SHE JUMPED OVERBOaRD!
SHE JUMPED?
THUNK
SIR? I THINK SHE'S STILL ON BOaRD...

CLUMP

SHE BE MOVIN AROUND DOWN BELOW!

CLUMP

CLUMP

CLUMP

CLUMP

CLOMP

CLOMP

CLOMP

CLOMP

here be THE HULL

WHAM

OW! BLAST!

BOOM

POMF

SCREE!

ALRIGHT YOU PINK-BRIEFED, SLACK-JAWED, SCURVY BUNCH OF SQUID SLIME!

WHAT DID YOU EXPECT WHEN YOU CAME ABOARD?

THIS IS A PIRATE SHIP, NOT SOME GUPOH ISLAND PLEASURE CRUISE!

AND ABOARD A PIRATE SHIP...

DEATH! DEATH!

THAT'S RIGHT CRAZY TED. MUTINY IS PUNISHABLE BY DEATH!

YAR.

HOOF!
UHN!
COME ON, THEN...
CHNG!
SHNK
HEH.
TIME TO CUT LOOSE THE MAIN-SAIL!

CLICK
NOW WHICH OF US IS FASTER D'YA THINK?
SIRS! THERE'S A MERCHANT GALLEON OFF THE STARBOARD BOW!
CLICK
THANKS POCKETS.
Whew...
AVAST! WOULD YE LOOK AT THAT!
FULLA GOLD I'LL WAGER!
THAT'S A HEAVILY-LADEN SHIP, THAT IS.
AYE! LOOK HOW LOW SHE RIDES IN THE WATER!
SHE BE A POOR MAN'S DREAM...

I WANT THAT SHIP.

YOUR HAT, CAP'N

THANKS, C.T. KEEP AN EYE ON THESE YAHOOS, WILL YE?

AYE!

ATTENTION CREW OF THE MOST DEADLY: ARM THE CANNONS, HOIST THE SAILS AND FULL TURN TO STARBOARD!

WE'VE A GALLEON TO PLUNDER!

AND SHOULD WE WIN THE DAY...

"ALL'S WELL THAT ENDS WELL SAYS I."

End

Story and Art
Johane Matte

CRASH!

ALMOST REACHED THE OCEAN!
BETTER THAN YESTERDAY.
POF!

I'M SURE THE LONGER WING SPAN IMPROVED THE PERFORMANCE, AND YOU COULD HAVE GONE EVEN FURTHER IF YOU HAD FLAPPED HARDER.

FLAP?!?
THESE THINGS ARE TOO LONG AND HEAVY TO FLAP! I COULD BARELY... "OW"...KEEP MY ARMS UP!

LET ME SEE...
I'M OKAY, I DON'T THINK IT'S BROKEN
OW!

NOT...ENOUGH... MUSCLES.

ACCORDING TO MY NEW CALCULATIONS, HUMAN POWERED FLIGHT MAY BE BEYOND OUR REACH. WE'LL HAVE TO SETTLE ON GLIDING.
JUST GLIDE? WHAT'S THE USE OF THAT?

WELL... LET'S SAY YOU ARE BEING PURSUED BY AN INVADING ARMY. YOU COULD RUN AWAY TOWARDS THE CLIFF ...

...AND JUMP OFF , YOUR PURSUERS UNABLE TO FOLLOW

EVEN FACING A MUCH LARGER FORCE, YOU'LL HAVE THE ELEMENT OF SURPRISE!
!!

BY THE TIME THEY REACT, YOU'LL HAVE SAFELY FLOWN AWAY FROM THE RANGE OF THEIR SPEARS
NYAH!

AUGH!

NICE SHOT.
THANKS.
SPLASH!

I DON'T THINK GLIDING WILL BE VERY POPULAR.

THAT'S IT.
THAT'S IT!
WE'LL USE A SAIL!

LOOK ICARUS, HOW AEOLUS, GOD OF WIND, PUSHES THIS GREAT BOAT WITH THE FORCE OF HIS BREATH!
PROPERLY HARNESSED, THE WIND'S MIGHTY POWER COULD LIFT A SINGLE MAN UP TO THE HEAVENS!
YEAH... THAT MIGHT WORK.

HMMM...IT SHOULD HAVE WORKED.
HE IS MUCH LIGHTER THAN A BOAT.

PLAN #38
MORE VELOCITY!
GET HIGH ENOUGH, MAY STAY IN THE AIR.
G=?
CRASH CRASH
GIANT BOW TOO EXPENSIVE
PLAN #69
BACK TO BASICS
BIRDS
200 OF THESE?
TWO OF THESE
JUST FEATHERS?
PLAN # 372
BEES
BAG
FLY TO GET OUT OF BAG
LIFT
4000 OF THOSE

PLAN 482
BAD!
TOO HEAVY
FEED HIM LESS
WINGX4?
DIET OF FLYING FISH?
I DID IT!
I GOT US SOME WORK!

TO DEADALUS, GREAT ENGINEER AND ARCHITECT...
THIS IS A BUILDING CONTRACT!
HEY, YOU SAID YOU NEEDED A GOOD PAYING JOB TO FINANCE YOUR RESEARCH. WELL, I GOT YOU ONE!

BUT DID YOU READ THIS? IT'S FROM KING MINOS, AND HE WANTS A WHOLE LABYRINTH! THAT'S GOING TO TAKE YEARS TO BUILD!
GOOD, I CAN USE THE VACATION.

"SIGH"
I REALLY BELIEVE I WAS GETTING CLOSE TO A BREAKTHROUGH...
STOP TALKING ABOUT WINGS AND START THINKING ABOUT WALLS.
LOTS AND LOTS OF WALLS!

WE WON'T NEED WINGS IN A LABYRINTH!
CHEER UP DAD! I HEAR CRETE IS A LOVELY PLACE. GREAT WEATHER, LOTS OF SUN...

Before my father died, he always taught me that I could live without using the magic that was given to me by The Gods.

He always said I can be powerful without them, if I really wanted to be.

Now that he's gone, I live with Raed, the leader of the militia known as "Keepers". He says using my magic is essential.

He tells me my powers are a part of who I am, and using them is the only way I will ever be successful.

But I still like to think that I can be powerful without them...

A Test for Cenri

BY AMY KIM GANTER

WPAP
SWOOSH
CHOMP
SPLURCH
urgh!
KICK

Use your powers, Cenri!! Use them now!!!
C'mon, boy! Don't make me rescue you again!

SWSHHH
SCKCH
KRACK
SCHNCK
hrgh...

Damn! He's hopeless!

KRRRKKRRKR

RRRRKRKRKRKKRKRKRR

HHWSHH

THNNK

Urgh!

hff hff

hff

hff

hff

ngh
hng
hff

hng
hgh
hgh

Why do I even bother?

Let's go home.

THIS WAS ALREADY MY TENTH BATTLE WITH THESE MONSTERS.

EACH ONE WAS A BIGGER DISAPPOINTMENT TO RAED THAN THE LAST.
I WISH I COULD'VE TOLD HIM HOW I WANTED TO DO THINGS DIFFERENTLY...
...BUT HE DOESN'T THINK I'M WORTH LISTENING TO.

I LEARNED THAT IT'S EASIER TO JUST BE SILENT.

I'm going. There's another attack.

No.

You're staying here.

I can't have a keeper following me around who refuses to use everything they've got.
...

You've made your choice.
Now live with it.

KRAKK
SLPP
SLPP
FFFWWSHH

This one sure likes to run away...
Too high...
Hnph. Very clever.

SKKCH
HHWWSSHHH
HWIK
SKRKK
HHRAAAAGH
Ergh!
If I can just pull it close enough to the ground...
!!!

FWTHNK
SLCKK
...!

SKUKK
HHWWSSHH

THAT LOOK...

JUST LIKE HIS FATHER'S!

The End

La Sonadora

by Joana Carneiro ★ Colours by Paulo Visgueiro

ONCE UPON A TIME THERE WERE FAERIES...

...WHO LIVED AS GODS OF THIS WORLD.

THEY LIVED CAREFREE LIVES...

NEITHER BEING BAD ENOUGH TO BE PUNISHED, OR GOOD ENOUGH TO BE SAVED.

THE FAERIES WERE RULED BY THEIR FAERIE GODMOTHER. SHE WAS THE QUEEN OF ALL LIGHT AND ENCHANTMENTS, AND WAS RESPECTED THROUGHOUT HER KINGDOM BY ALL LIVING CREATURES.

FOR A TIME, SHE WAS A FAIR RULER.

BUT AS TIME PASSED ON, THE FAERIE QUEEN BECAME CORRUPTED BY THE POWER BESTOWED UPON HER BY THE STARS.

HER GREED GREW UNTIL SHE DESIRED ALL THE LIGHT FROM THE STARS FOR HERSELF.

AND SO SHE COMMANDED HER DAUGHTERS TO RETRIEVE IT FOR HER:
THE THREE FAERIE PRINCESSES.

SHE CHOSE THEM BECAUSE THEY WERE STILL PURE AND UNTOUCHED BY THE STARS POWER.

TO HELP THEM ON THEIR QUEST, THE QUEEN GAVE THE PRINCESSES A MAGIC LANTERN TO COLLECT THE LIGHT OF THE STARS.

OOOOOOH!

"THE LIGHT OF THE STARS, MOM?"
ASKED THE FIRST PRINCESS.

"AM I ALLOWED TO DO SO?"

SHE WAS VERY SCARED.

SO SHE FLEW TOWARDS THE VERY FIRST STAR,
AND TOOK ONLY HALF OF ITS LIGHT.

BUT IT WAS NOT ENOUGH.

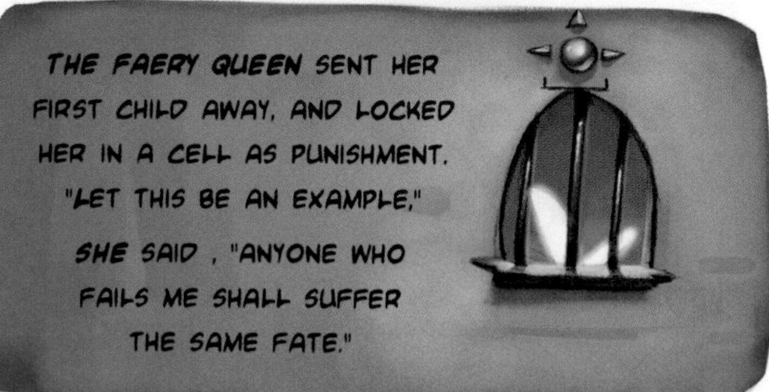

THE FAERY QUEEN SENT HER FIRST CHILD AWAY, AND LOCKED HER IN A CELL AS PUNISHMENT. "LET THIS BE AN EXAMPLE," SHE SAID , "ANYONE WHO FAILS ME SHALL SUFFER THE SAME FATE."

SHE SEARCHED FOR THE BRIGHTEST STAR IN THE SKY...

YEAP!!!

...BUT THE LIGHT WAS FAR BRIGHTER THAN SHE EVER EXPECTED.
AWWww!!!
WITH THE MISFORTUNE THAT BEFELL HER TWO SISTERS, THE LAST CHILD,
"GLINDA"
BECAME DOUBTFUL AND FEARED FOR HER OWN FATE.

GLINDA WAS THE YOUNGEST AND THE LAST OF THE THREE PRINCESSES LEFT TO PURSUETHE LIGHT OF THE STARS. UNLIKE HER OTHER SISTERS, GLINDA WAS BORN WITHOUT WINGS, BUT SHE WAS GIFTED WITH THE ABILITY TO DREAM DURING THE DAYTIME.
WHEN SHE WAS A CHILD, GLINDA WOULD OFTEN DREAM OF FLYING UP TO THE STARS. HER MOTHER ONCE TOLD GLINDA THAT HER WINGS COULD ONLY RISE FROM HER SHOULDERS WHEN THE TIME WAS RIGHT, AND THAT SHE WOULD HAVE TO OVERCOME GREAT ADVERSITY TO DO SO. ONLY THEN WOULD SHE BECOME A TRUE FAERIE SPIRIT.
TIME PASSED, BUT GLINDA WAS NEVER BLESSED WITH WINGS. UNABLE TO FLY, SHE HAD NO OTHER CHOICE BUT TO ASK FOR SPIRITUAL GUIDANCE.
GLINDA SOUGHT OUT THE GREAT FOREST GOD FOR HELP.

BUMP!
HEY!!!

OOOOOHH!!!

YOU MUST BE THE FOREST GOD!

CAN YOU HELP ME COLLECT THE LIGHT OF A STAR FROM THE SKY?

"IF YOU GET ME A NUT, I WILL GET YOU WHAT YOU WISH FOR,"
SAID THE FOREST GOD...

HUUUMPFT!

HUH?

OH NO!

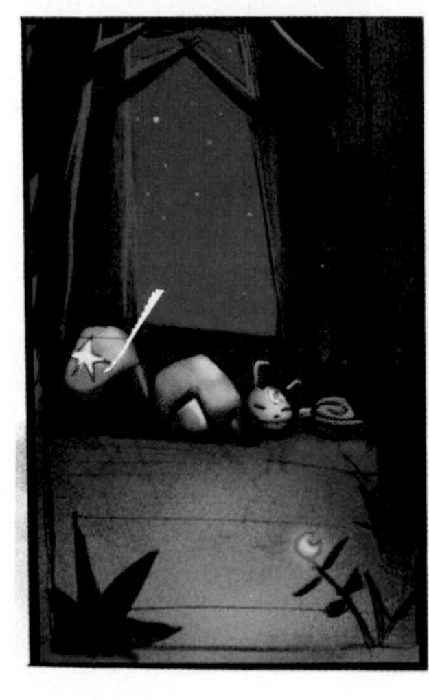

COME BACK!

BUT LUCK NEVER TRULY LEAVES THOSE WHO HAVE HOPE.

GLINDA HAD FOUND HERSELF A FALLEN STAR, WITH WHICH SHE COULD COLLECT ALL THE LIGHT SHE WISHED FOR.

HOWEVER, HER JOURNEY WAS NOT YET AT AN END. WHILE GLINDA WAS IN THE FOREST SEARCHING FOR HER STAR, THE FAERIE QUEEN HAD GONE MAD, KEEPING THE OTHER TWO PRINCESSES AS HER PRISONERS.

RETURNING TO HER VILLAGE, GLINDA HAD TO FIND A WAY TO DELIVER THE LIGHT TO HER MOTHER AND FREE HER SISTERS FROM THEIR IMPRISONMENT.

GIVE IT TO ME!

HERE MOM!!!

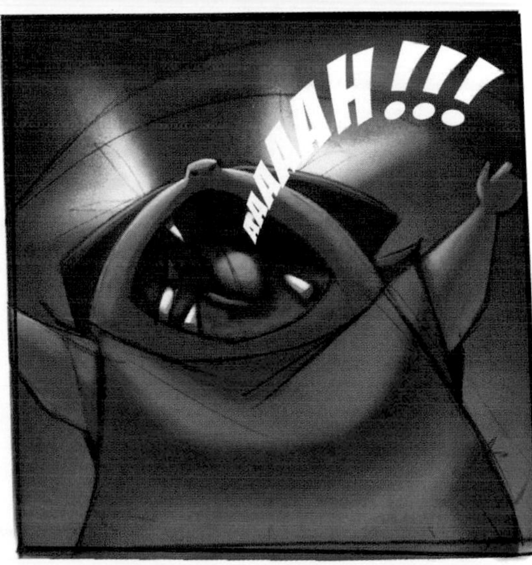
RAAAAAH!!!

THE LIGHT OF THE STAR BLINDED THE EVIL QUEEN,

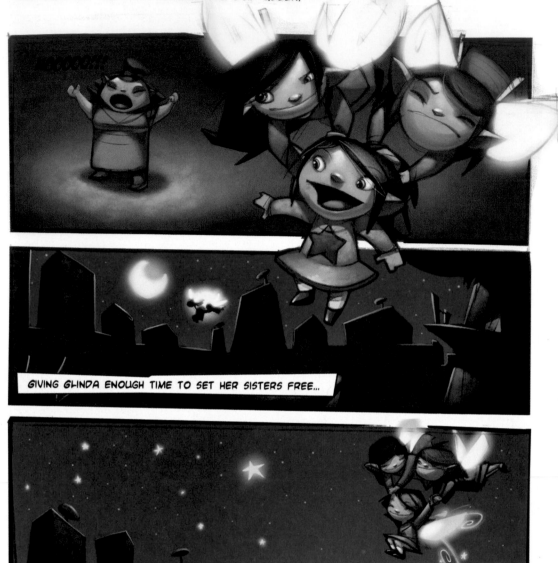

GIVING GLINDA ENOUGH TIME TO SET HER SISTERS FREE...

AND SO IT WAS THAT GLINDA'S WINGS GREW SO BIG THAT SHE NOW FLIES AS HIGH AS HER DREAMS ONCE WERE.
FIN

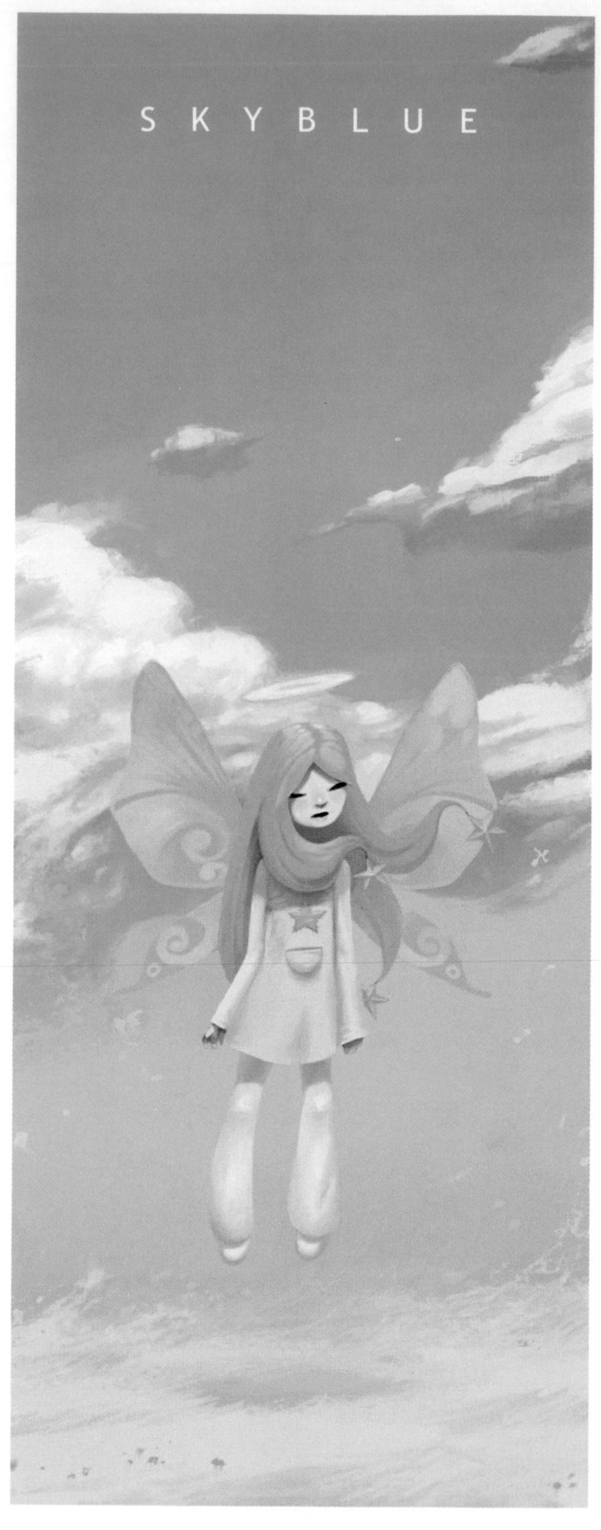

art-**KNESS**(www.kness.net)
story-**M.FORICHON**(matthieu.forichon.free.fr)
translation-**CLAIRE DE MASSĒ**
covercolor-**MADE**(www.m4de.com)

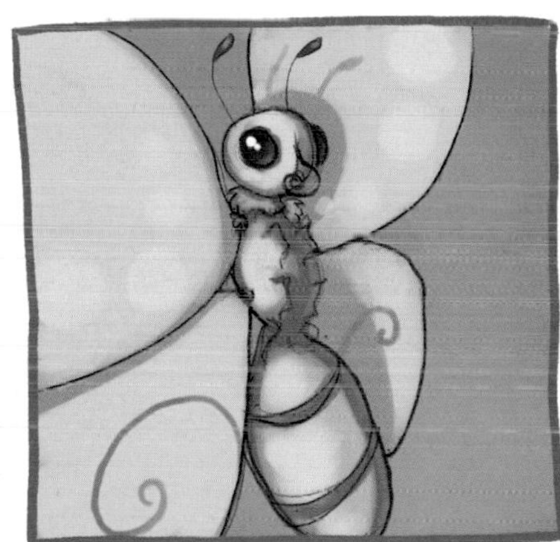

How tiny they are !

Becoming bigger when they touch my nose ...
and smaller when they land on my toes.

Isn't the sky wide enough to shelter all my butterflies ?

If they remained the same
size as on my nose ...

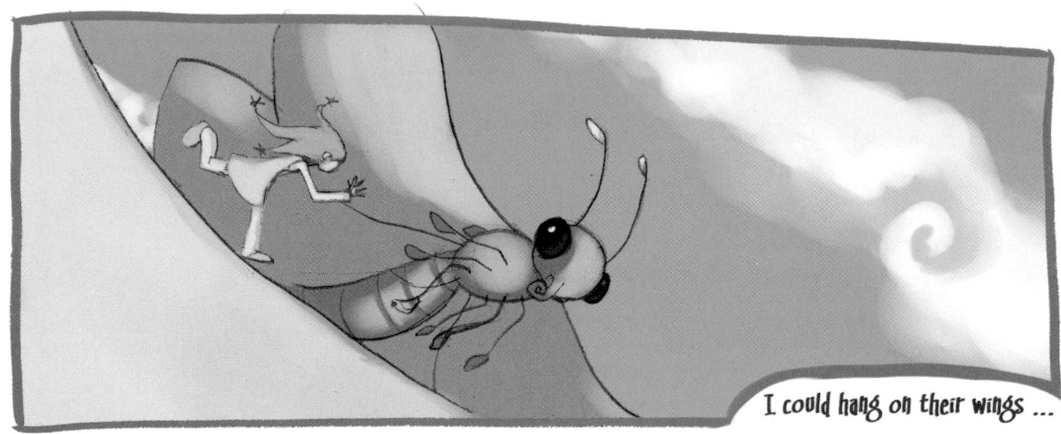
I could hang on their wings ...

To chase those ugly planes away

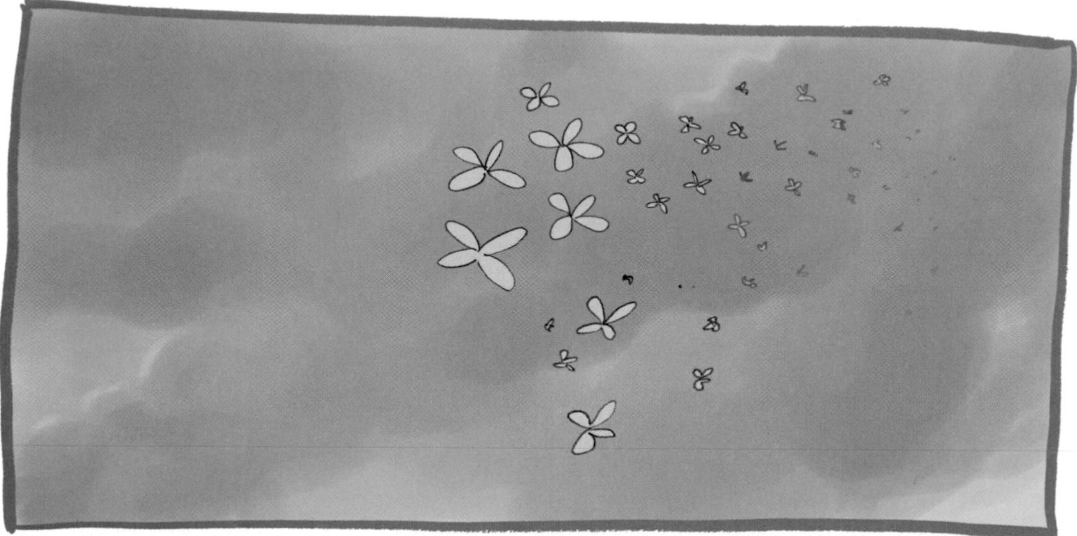

And see my parents again.

In my pockets,

I would bring pieces of clouds back

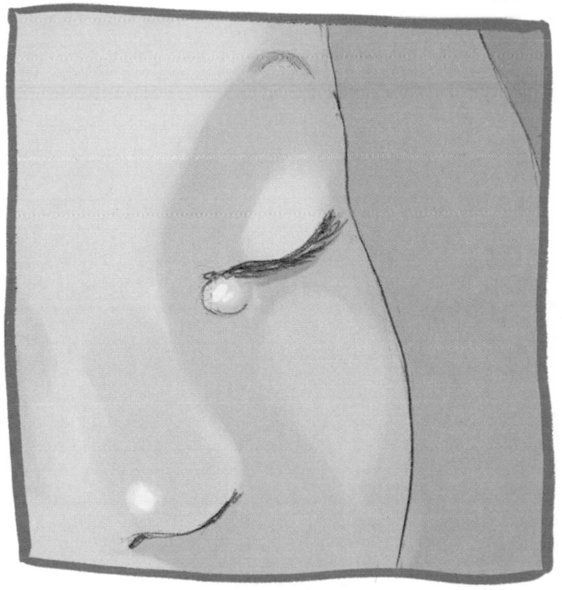

To dry our tears.

And stop their guns.

BÉISBOL

THE STORY OF FRANCISCO SANCHEZ

STORY AND ART
RICHARD POSE

COLORS
ISRAEL SANCHEZ

I CAN'T BELIEVE I'M ACTUALLY HERE...

. . . THE BIG LEAGUES
KINGFISH
I USED TO DREAM ABOUT THIS DAY...

BIG LEAGUE HITTERS...
POP UP.

BIG LEAGUE COACHES...

...NOW ALL I DREAM ABOUT ARE MY FRIENDS, MY FAMILY, AND MY COUNTRY...

BIG LEAGUE HOT DOGS...

AND...
YOU SUCK!
BUM!
GOOD FER NOTHIN'!
BIG LEAGUE FANS!

...I WISH HE WERE HERE RIGHT NOW...

SEÑOR ARMANDO GONZALEZ
¿PERO PORQUE NO ME DEJAS JUGAR?

EL COTORRO, CUBA... MANY YEARS AGO
DAMN IT FRANCISCO, YOU ASK ME THE SAME QUESTION EVERYDAY...
...I ALREADY TOLD YOU, YOU'RE TOO YOUNG TO PLAY WITH US.
BUT I'M OLDER TODAY...
NO.
BUT...

¡NO!
GO HOME AND LEAVE ME ALONE ¿OK?!

I JUST WANNA PLAY...
FLICK

BUMP

¡OYE FRANCISCO!
¿CAN YOU BRING THAT BACK TO ME?

THANKS...
...OLD THING ROLLED RIGHT OFF THE TABLE.
SO... I NOTICED YOUR BROTHER DIDN'T LET YOU PLAY TODAY...

BUT I BET YOU'RE GONNA TRY AGAIN TOMORROW, ¿EH?
¿FRANCISCO?
...
¿FRANCISCO?

¡FRANCISCO!
YOINK

OH SORRY SEÑOR GONZALEZ.
THAT'S FINE,... BUT ¿IS EVERYTHING OK? YOU WERE STARING AT THIS BASEBALL LIKE YOU'D NEVER SEEN ONE BEFORE.
¿WHAT'S WRONG?
OH, NOTHINGS WRONG, IT'S JUST...

I'VE NEVER SEEN A REAL BASEBALL...
...IT'S A PEARL COMPARED TO THE "BALL" MY BROTHER USES.

MY BROTHER'S BASEBALL
GENUINE BLACK TAPE HIDE
LOPSIDED
EXPOSED STRINGS

OK, I'LL MAKE YOU A DEAL...
IF YOU COME OVER ALL THIS WEEK AND KEEP ME COMPANY,
I WILL GIVE YOU THIS BASEBALL.
¿HOW'S THAT SOUND?

¡¡SOUNDS GREAT!!
¿BUT... ARE YOU SERIOUS?

¿DO WE HAVE A DEAL?

¡DEAL!

¿YOU WANT TO PLAY BASEBALL, RIGHT?
YES.
OK, THEN I SUGGEST YOU START TO TOUGHEN UP THAT GRIP OF YOURS...
AND EAT LOTS OF CARROTS WHILE YOU'RE AT IT...

BECAUSE STRONG WRISTS AND GOOD EYES ARE TWO OF THE MOST IMPORTANT...

YO
MÍ HERMANO
BLAH BLAH BLAH

...SO THEN YOU CAN TURN ON A FASTBALL BETTER AND ADJUST TO THE CURVEBALL IF...
WHOOSH

OK, GO ON, GET OUTTA HERE, I NEED A LITTLE SIESTA.
OK SEÑOR GONZALEZ... THANK YOU SEÑOR GONZALEZ.
DON'T THANK ME, I HAVEN'T GIVEN YOU ANYTHING YET...

GO HOME, I'LL SEE YOU HERE BRIGHT AND EARLY TOMORROW.
HASTA MAÑANA SEÑOR.
¡MAMÁ MAMÁ!
¿¡GUESS WHAT SEÑOR GONZALEZ IS GONNA GIVE ME!?

LUNES
HOLA SEÑOR GONZALEZ... ¿QUE VAMOS HACER HOY? YO QUIE...

SHHHH

MARTES

MIERCOLES
ZZZZZZZZZZZ

TAP TAP

JUEVES

VIERNES
...

...

¿¡QUÉ!?

MY BROTHER SAID I CAN GO PLAY WITH HIM TODAY IF I BRING THE BASEBALL WITH ME... BUT HE NEEDS IT RIGHT NOW... AND THIS IS THE FIRST TIME HE'S EVER SAID I COULD PLAY... ITS MY ONLY CHANCE.

¿SO CAN YOU GIVE ME THE BALL SO I CAN GO PLAY?

THAT'S NOT THE DEAL WE SHOOK ON...
I KNOW, BUT...
YOU STILL OWE ME TODAY, THEN YOU GET THE BALL.
BUT...
¿IS BASEBALL MORE IMPORTANT THAN YOUR WORD?... ... ¿YOUR HONOR?
.....
YOUR ANSWER SHOULD BE 'NO'
LISTEN, I AM HOLDING TO OUR AGREEMENT... IF YOU WANT TO LEAVE NOW, I WILL NOT GIVE YOU THE BASEBALL!

THERE'S YOUR BROTHER...
... I THINK YOU MIGHT WANT TO LET HIM KNOW WHAT'S GOING ON.

SKREEEEE

?

¿OH, SO YOU WANT TO SIT THERE ALL ANGRY AND POUTY?
¿YOU DON'T THINK THERE WILL BE ANOTHER DAY TO PLAY BASEBALL?

FINE THEN... I LIKE YOU BETTER WHEN YOU ARE QUIET ANYWAYS.
?
SKREEEEEEEEE...

¡¡ALL I WANTED TO DO WAS PLAY!! ... ¡¡BUT YOU WOULDN'T LET ME!!

WITH THIS BASEBALL, YOU'LL HAVE THE FREEDOM TO DECIDE WHERE AND WHEN YOU WANT TO PLAY...
NOW, YOU CAN BE AS ANGRY AS YOU WANT, BUT I WILL KEEP MY WORD WITH YOU,...

...IN A FEW HOURS I WILL HAND YOU THIS BASEBALL.
UNTIL THEN, WE CAN SIT IN SILENCE IF YOU WISH.

I'M SORRY SEÑOR GONZALEZ...
I DIDN'T MEAN TO YELL, BUT IT'S JUST. WELL, I LOVE BASEBALL SO MUCH.
YOU WOULDN'T UNDERSTAND, I MEAN... YOU DON'T EVEN LIKE BASEBALL.

WAIT A SECOND... ¿YOU THINK I DON'T LIKE BASEBALL?
YOU NEVER TALK ABOUT IT...
YOU NEVER ASK...

¿DO YOU LIKE TONY PEREZ?

PEREZ IS QUITE GOOD.
YEAH, HE'S MY FAVORITE.

¿DO YOU HAVE A FAVORITE PLAYER?

¿DO I HAVE A FAVORITE PLAYER?...
...HMMM, I SUPPOSE I HAVE A FEW...

BUT, THEY PLAYED A LOOONG TIME AGO...
SEÑOR GONZALEZ
WHEN I WAS VERY YOUNG.

ANYWAYS, ¿HAVE YOU EVER HEARD OF "THE PRIDE OF HAVANA," ADOLFO LUQUE?
NO... ¿WAS HE GOOD?

HEHE... I THINK SO, HE PITCHED FOR 20 YEARS IN THE MAJOR LEAGUES... AND IN 1923 HE LED ALL THE MAJORS WITH A 27-8 WIN/LOSS RECORD AND A 1.93 ERA.

LUQUE ALSO PLAYED 22 YEARS OF WINTER-BALL RIGHT HERE... IT'S STRANGE, BUT EVERYTIME I FACED HIM, HE USED TO KNOCK ME DOWN WITH THE FIRST PITCH...
¡ACK!
WAIT, WAIT, WAIT... ¿ARE YOU SAYING YOU USED TO PLAY BASE-BALL?!

YEP...
MANDO GONZALEZ
CIENFUEGO

WHAT TEAM DID YOU PLAY FOR? ¿HO MANY HOME RUNS DID YOU HIT? ¿WHO ELSE DID YOU PLAY WITH? ¿HOW LON DID YOU PLAY? ¿DID YOU STEAL BASE ¿HOW MANY? ¿HOW MANY TIMES DID YOU GET HIT BY THE PITCH? ¿WHAT POSITION DID YOU PLAY? ¿INFIELD? ¿OUTFIELD? ¿WHY WON'T YOU SPEAK ¡¡TELL ME!!

CALM DOWN, HEHE... ONE QUESTION AT A TIME.

I SAT AND LISTENED TO SEÑOR GONZALEZ'S STORIES FOR HOURS... I FORGOT ALL ABOUT MY BROTHER...
¡HECK, I WAS SO EXCITED, I FORGOT TO TAKE MY BASEBALL HOME!

BUT THAT WAS OK, HE TAUGHT ME MORE THAN AN OLD PIECE OF LEATHER AND STRINGS COULD...

KID!!
?
GRAB A STICK!

YOU SPEAK ENGLISH?!
JES...
WELL THEN, YOU HEARD ME... YER UP!

SEÑOR GONZALEZ GAVE ME ADVICE THROUGHOUT MY YOUTH SO THAT LIFE WOULD BE A LITTLE LESS...
...COMPLICATED

LIKE HOW TO TELL WRONG...

...FROM RIGHT!

AND TO MAKE SURE YOUR HANDS ARE ALWAYS CLEAN...

...AND YOUR UNIFORM ALWAYS DIRTY...

...AND HE TAUGHT ME TO FIX A 1954 CHEVY WITH PARTS FROM A TOASTER, A BOAT MOTOR, AND A 10-SPEED BIKE...

HE WOULD ALWAYS TELL ME TO RESPECT MY ELDERS...
HELLO SEÑOR UMPIRE.

SHOVE IT! YA KISSASS.
MORE THAN ALL THAT HE TAUGHT ME TO PLAY BASEBALL.

LIKE HOW TO TELL IF A PITCHER IS THROWING A FASTBALL OR A CURVE...

STEEERIKE!!!
UNFORTUNATELY, HE COULDN'T TEACH ME TO HIT IT.
TIME OUT SEÑOR.
TIME!
THANK EH-JOU
MORE THAN ANYTHING I JUST LIKED SITTING THERE AND LISTENING TO HIS OLD STORIES.
HE WOULD TELL ME ABOUT ALL THE GREAT GAMES, TEAMS, AND PLAYERS...
DOLF LUQUE PLAYED IN THE MAJORS UNTIL HE WAS 45... HE RACKED UP 194 WINS IN THE U.S.A. AND ANOTHER 106 WINS IN CUBA.
MARTÍN DIHIGO WAS KNOWN AS THE BEST ALL-AROUND PLAYER IN ALL OF BASEBALL.
DIHIGO WON BATTING, HOMERUN, AND PITCHING TITLES IN HIS CAREER AND HE EXCELLED AT EIGHT DEFENSIVE POSITIONS...
EL IMMORTAL
CIENFUEGOS
DIHIGO IS ENSHRINED IN THE CUBAN, MEXICAN, VENEZUELAN, AND U.S. BASEBALL HALLS OF FAME.
1 2 3
JONRÓN
IN 1920, CRISTOBAL TORRIENTE SMASHED THREE HOME RUNS IN ONE GAME VERSUS A TEAM OF MAJOR LEAGUERS LED BY THE GREAT BABE RUTH!
AS SEÑOR GONZALEZ TOLD ME TALES OF THESE CUBAN GIANTS, I WOULD DREAM... DREAM OF PLAYING BASEBALL.

AT AGE 19, I FOUND MYSELF PLAYING FOR THE POPULAR IDUSTRIALES BÉISBOL CLUB.
F. SANCHEZ
2DA B

I WAS ECSTATIC TO BE PLAYING PROFESSIONAL BASEBALL...

AND I DIDN'T WASTE MY OPPORTUNITY.

EACH NIGHT I WOULD RACE BACK AND GIVE SEÑOR GONZALEZ A RECAP OF THE GAME...
I COULDN'T BE HAPPIER... LIFE COULDN'T BE BETTER...

...¿OR COULD IT?
DON'T GET ME WRONG, I WAS VERY HAPPY IN CUBA, BUT...
...AS A BALLPLAYER, ONE ALWAYS WONDERS HOW HE WOULD PERFORM IN THE BIG LEAGUES...

... I SHOULD HAVE KEPT THAT THOUGHT TO MYSELF.
OYE CHEO...
¿YOU EVER WONDER ABOUT PLAYING IN THE UNITED STATES?
I HAD A DREAM LAST NIGHT, I WAS FACING ROGER CLEMENS...

NO COMPAÑERO...
I DON'T THINK OF THOSE THINGS...
EXCUSE ME FOR A MINUTE...

¿HELLO?
I HAVE SOME INFORMATION FOR YOU...

THE NEXT DAY, I FOUND MY LOCKER EMPTIED OUT...
PÉREZ
GARCIA

I WAS KICKED OFF THE TEAM...
ENTRADA DE PELOTEROS
...AND BANNED FROM BASEBALL.

LIFE HAD SUDDENLY TURNED INTO A NIGHTMARE...
EVERYWHERE I WENT, GOVERNMENT AGENTS FOLLOWED ME...

FOR WEEKS I FOUND MYSELF UNABLE TO SLEEP.. UNWILLING TO DREAM...
IT WAS RIDICULOUS, ALL I WANTED TO DO WAS PLAY BASEBALL, AND NOW THE GOVERNMENT WOULDN'T LET ME...

ONE RESTLESS NIGHT I FOUND MYSELF WANDERING THE STREETS OF HAVANA...

UNTIL...

KNOCK
KNOCK
KNOCK

¡FRANCISCO! ¿QUÉ TAL?
SEÑOR GONZALEZ, I THINK I HAVE SERIOUS PROBLEMS.

AHH...¿YOU ARE HAVING TROUBLE HITTING THE CURVEBALL?
REMEMBER... EVEN IF YOUR KNEES BUCKLE, YOU NEED TO DIG IN DEEPER ON THE NEXT PITCH...

...NEVER LET ANYONE TAKE CONTROL OF YOUR AT-BATS... YOU GET TOO FEW IN LIFE.
THIS ISN'T ABOUT CURVEBALLS SEÑOR...
¿¡OH REALLY!? HMM, I COULD HAVE SWORN IT WAS...
WELL, ANYWAYS...

...HERE YOU GO.
¿WHAT'S THIS?
JUST SIT DOWN AND OPEN IT FRANCISCO.

I KNOW YOU PROBABLY HAVE TONS OF THESE LITTERING YOUR HOME, BUT I MADE A PROMISE TO YOU A WHILE AGO...

... AND A MAN SHOULDN'T BREAK HIS WORD...

¿WHAT'S WRONG? I KNOW I SHOULD HAVE GIVEN IT TO YOU A LONG TIME AGO...
NO, IT'S NOT THAT, IT'S JUST...

WELL, THANK YOU SEÑOR GONZALEZ.

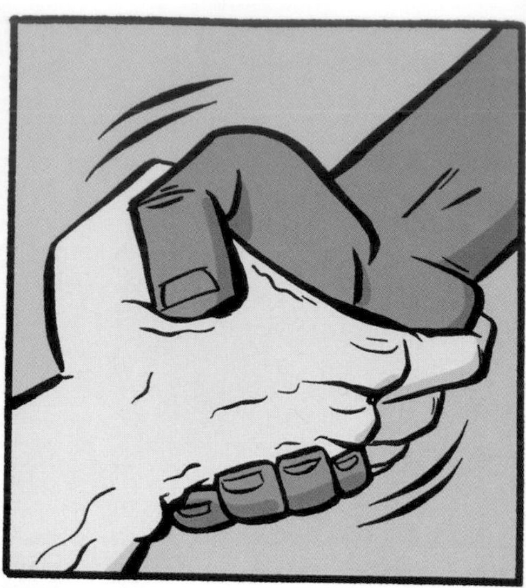

I NEED TO RUN NOW SEÑOR, THANK YOU AGAIN.
DE NADA MIJO.

HASTA LUEGO FRANCISCO.

GOOD BYE.

¡HOLA SEÑOR!

¿OYE SEÑOR, DO YOU KNOW WHERE FRANCISCO IS?

¿FRANCISCO?...

¿DON'T YOU KNOW...?

CURVE.

... HE'S PLAYING BASEBALL TODAY.
CRACK

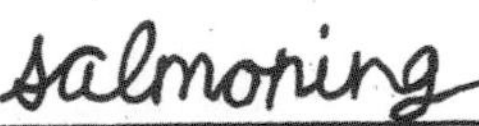

salmoning
by vera brosgol

We went to mississauga to see the salmon spawning.

It was late in the season, so the river bottom was littered with the bodies of fish who'd died from exhaustion.
Poke

some of the salmon had taken a wrong turn and were struggling against the water from a sewer...
...instead of up the correct current to the spawning grounds.

These fish were going to fight against the wrong current until they couldn't anymore – then sink and die.

I need to stop applying symbolic meaning to everything I see.

FLIGHT VOLUME TWO CREW

from left to right:

1st row: Doug TenNapel, Rodolphe Guenoden, Herval, Hope Larson, Clio Chiang, Ben Hatke **2nd row:** Michel Gagné, Doug Holgate, Amy Kim Ganter, Matthew Woodson, Richard Pose, Neil Babra **3rd row:** Phil Craven, Bannister, Rad Sechrist, Jeff Smith, Giuseppe Ferrario, Sonny Liew **4th row:** Kean Soo, Don Hertzfeldt, Ryan Sias, Becky Cloonan, Jake Parker, Vera Brosgol **5th row:** Johane Matte, Kness, Jen Wang, Chris Appelhans, Catia Chien, Khang Le **6th row:** Justin Ridge, Kazu Kibuishi, Joana Carneiro

Born in 1980, **Amy Kim Ganter** has worked in the past as a freelance animator and illustrator. She is now working on a graphic novel with Tokyopop called *Sorcerers and Secretaries*, and is also the creator of the epic fantasy comic *Reman Mythology*, currently being serialized on the web. She enjoys mint green tea and staring into space. www.felaxx.com

Bannister was born in 1973 and lives as an illustrator/cartoonist/Flash animator near the French Alps with his girlfriend. His first book, *Félicité Bonaventure*, was published in France in 2004. He is currently working on various projects both in France and overseas, and hopes his drawings will one day help him to buy a house. www.bannister.fr

At the time of this writing, **Becky Cloonan** is perhaps best known for her artwork on *Demo*. In a few years, who really knows what people will remember her for? "More comics," she hopes. www.estrigious.com/becky/

Ben Hatke is a grizzled, crotchety chicken farmer living in Virginia with his charming wife and two children. He is a freelance illustrator and has worked on various comics and children's books, including the recent *Angel in the Waters*. www.househatke.com / www.zitaspacegirl.com

Catia Chien is a concept artist, children's book illustrator and gallery artist. She loves good stories and also finds time to doodle t-shirt designs, create vintage boxes, and occasionally sews one-of-a-kind scary plush toys for some of her not so lucky friends. www.catiachien.com

Chris Appelhans (cover illustration) currently works as a visual development artist on the film *Monster House* at Sony Imageworks. He is also the creator of the comic strip *Frank and Frank*. www.froghatstudios.com

Clio Chiang is on the way to finishing her time in the Capilano College Animation program and hopes to enter the work force soon afterwards. She is currently obsessed with turning animals into construction vehicles and making goldfish bounce. www.cliochiang.com

Don Hertzfeldt has been drawing badly since he was little, and has wanted to make films for as long as he can remember. His animated films have collectively been seen in over a thousand film festivals and theatrical venues around the world. His film *Rejected* was nominated for an Oscar in 2001, and in 2003, he created "The Animation Show" with Mike Judge, an annual theatrical tour of the world's best animated short films. www.bitterfilms.com

Doug Holgate is a freelance illustrator and cartoonist who is currently working on a series of children's books, as well as *Heidi Hyperwarp* for Image Comics, a graphic novel due out later in 2005. He lives in Melbourne, Australia and his palatial grounds are open to the public, 9-5 Monday through Friday. www.skullduggery.com.au

Doug TenNapel's comic work includes *GEAR*, *Creature Tech, Tommysaurus Rex* and *Earthboy Jacobus*. He based "Solomon Fix" on the fancy Englishmen he worked with while creating *Earthworm Jim*. He lives in Glendale with his tolerant wife, pert daughter, noble son and coming soon baby. www.tennapel.com

Giuseppe Ferrario lives in Milano, Italy and has worked as a freelance illustrator and cartoonist for the past 14 years, working with such characters as Bugs Bunny, Fred Flintstone, Geronimo Stilton, Mickey Mouse, and Scooby Doo. In 2002, he established Studio EFFIGIE, a cartoon and graphics studio, and is currently developing a TV series with a French broadcaster. www.giuseppeferrario.com

Born in 1966 in Rouen, France and entirely self-taught, **Herval** has worked in the past for advertising agencies as a graphic designer and artistic director. Currently a freelance artist and illustrator, his published work includes a collection of short stories, BD Clip, an all-ages graphic novel, *Captain Pirate*, and a collection of pin-ups called Drôles de Pin-up. mapage.noos.fr/herval/

Hope Larson graduated from the School of the Art Institute of Chicago in 2004 and promptly immigrated to Canada, where she now lives with her husband and two cats. One half of the *Secret Friend Society*, she is currently hard at work finishing up her first graphic novel, *Salamander Dream*. www.hopelarson.com / www.secretfriendsociety.com//

Jake Parker dropped out of school to pursue a career in the animation industry, and he now works as an art director for Reel FX Creative Studios. He lives in Dallas with his wife Alison and two children, Tate and Lucy. His free time is spent working on projects like FLIGHT. www.agent44.com

Jeff Smith is the author of the independent epic comic series *Bone*. Jeff currently resides in Columbus, Ohio with his wife and business partner, Vijaya. Upcoming projects include *Captain Marvel: Monster Society of Evil* for DC Comics, and *BIG, BIG* for Cartoon Books. www.boneville.com

Jen Wang celebrates her 21st birthday on the eve of this book's publishing. She resides in San Francisco where she studies political and social science by day and draws cartoons by night. She likes big cities, soy, biological mishaps, and stars. www.jenwang.net

Joana Carneiro is 25 years old and was born and raised in Rio de Janeiro, Brazil. She has studied graphic design and currently works as a concept artist and illustrator for SeagullsFly. Joana is also developing a children's book called *Perninhas de Plantas*, to be released in 2005. www.joanacarneiro.com

Johane Matte works in animation and video games, will gladly organise your wine and cheese parties, and will sometimes manage to continue drawing her comic *Horus*. www.qosmiq.com/rufftoon/

Justin Ridge was born in 1981, and after graduating from CSU Fullerton, he has worked at Nickelodeon Studios as a character designer on *Fatherhood*, and is currently an Assistant Director for *Avatar: The Last Airbender*. He is also working on a top-secret film noir graphic novel and posts a lot of silly drawings on his website. www.justinridge.com

Kazu Kibuishi is the editor and art director of FLIGHT Volume Two. He recently completed his first graphic novel, *Daisy Kutter - The Last Train*, and is currently at work on his next book, which will be serialized in the pages of FLIGHT. www.boltcity.com

Kean Soo has a degree in electrical engineering, and couldn't be happier that he is wasting his education by drawing comics. He continues to document his life with his autobiographical *Exit Music* comics, and he is also the other half of the *Secret Friend Society*, where his first full-length comic *Jellaby* is being serialized on the web.www.keaner.net / www.secretfriendsociety.com

Khang Le is currently working as a freelance concept artist for video games and films. When he's not painting fantasy worlds or drawing his FLIGHT comic, he is most likely eating a steaming bowl of noodles. www.khangle.net

Kness is a 25 year-old self-taught freelance illustrator and colorist living in Paris, France. She secretly wants to be a gecko, but then that would mean she wouldn't be drawing anymore. www.kness.net

Matthew Woodson is a freelance illustator who lives in Chicago with his girlfriend and a menagerie of baneful animals. He is currently working on a project for Top Shelf and will eventually compile his own work for a short story collection, post- graduation from the School of the Art Intistute of Chicago, in early summer 2005.

Michel Gagné was born in Quebéc, Canada and has had a highly successful career drawing characters and special effects for animated and live-action feature films such as *The Iron Giant* and *Osmosis Jones*. His independent short film, *Prelude to Eden*, is a favorite among animation students and teachers, and has played in festivals throughout the world. Michel and his wife created Gagné International Press in 1998, and he has been writing, illustrating, and publishing books and comics ever since. www.gagneint.com

Neil Babra, a native son of Pennsylvania, is reasonably well educated and hygienic, except for an occasional hermit beard. www.neilcomics.com

Phil Craven is 27 and hails from the state of Georgia, where he went to grad school at the Savannah College of Art and Design. These days, Phil draws storyboards for DreamWorks Animation. He maintains a keen interest in soccer and cereal. www.bluepillow.net

Rad Sechrist is a 24 year old freelance illustrator living in LA with his wife Mandy. Along with working on Flight, Rad also does a webcomic called *Beneath the Leaves* on his website. www.radsechrist.com

Richard Pose graduated from CSU Fullerton and is one of the co-creators of the self-published comic *Smoke*. He is 26 and loves baseball -- especially his Los Angeles Angels. www.richardpose.com

Rodolphe Guenoden studied animation at the Gobelins in Paris, and has worked for 15 years in the animation industry as a 2D animator and storyboard artist on such films as *Fievel Goes West*, *Prince of Egypt*, *Road to El Dorado*, and *Sinbad*. Rodolphe lives in Los Angeles with his wife, their kids, and a cat. He loves drawing women, and has always wanted to draw comics. www.rodguen.com

Ryan Sias draws storyboards by day and comics by night. He has worked on the Oscar- winning documentary *Bowling for Columbine* and 20th Century Fox's *Robots*. Ryan is currently working on various children's books and his all-ages graphic novel, Silent Kimbly. www.ryansias.com / www.silentkimbly.com

Sonny Liew has worked on computer games and drawn comics like the Xeric- winning *Malinky Robot* and DC Vertigo's *My Faith in Frankie*. He lives in Singapore, where he sleeps with the fishes. www.sonnyliew.com

Vera Brosgol is in her final year of animation at Sheridan College, and has worked as an artist on Oni's *Hopeless Savages*. She never had a piece of fresh fruit until she was twenty, and it was a lime. She still takes the existence of peaches on hearsay. www.verabee.com

---

Israel Sanchez (colorist, "Beisbol") studied art at Cal State Fullerton and he now lives in La Habra, California, where he trains for regional foosball competitions. www.israelsanchez.com

Paulo Visgueiro (colorist, "La Sonadora") is a designer and illustrator, currently working as an art director in his home town of Rio de Janeiro, Brazil. www.visgueiro.com

Steve Hamaker (colorist, "Sirius and Betelgeuse") was a toy designer when he met Jeff Smith in 1998. After working on the Bone toys with Cartoon Books, Steve is currently coloring the 1300 pages of *Bone* for Scholastic, in addition to an upcoming *Shazam* mini-series for DC comics. He self-published a comic book called "Fish N Chips," and loves his job!

Vasilis Lolos (co-writer, "Heads Up") was born in 1981, in Athens, Greece. After switching schools several times, he solemnly devoted his life to comics. Vasilis' graphic novel, *Generator*, was published in 2004, and he is currently working on his first international book.

Aris, (writer, "Impossible") born in Toulouse, entered the comics field through several art studios. With Garrigue he created Le Studio, an association that published the annual magazine Azimuts. At the Salon de Colomiers, Aris met Christophe Gibelin, with whom he started the series 'Le Vieux Ferrand' in 2000.

Here is an email we received around the time we completed Flight Volume One. We weren't able to get Jordan's cloud in time for the first book, so we're proud to premiere it in Flight Volume Two...

could i join in on the comic FLIGHT? it doesn't need to be big at all, it could be drawin a cloud... it doesn't matter. i just want to be part of something of all that these great artist that ive admired for a long time. i'm 14, ut i think i can draw a cloud just as good anyone else. so if i could be part of this, i dontneed money or anything, i just want in.

thanks
Jordan N. of seattle

A FLIGHT comic by our friend Ben Zhu, owner of Nucleus
www.gallerynucleus.com

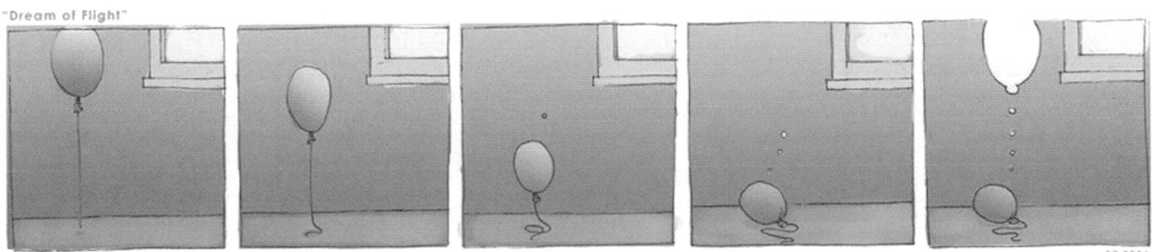